The Internationalists

Business Strategies for Globalization

Catherine W. Scherer

BookPartners
Wilsonville, Oregon

Library of Congress Cataloging-in-Publication Data

Scherer, Catherine, 1942–
    The internationalists : strategies for globalization / Catherine Scherer.
        p.   cm.
    Includes bibliographical references and index.
    ISBN 1-58151-040-3 (alk. paper)
    1. International business enterprises—Management.
    2. International business enterprises—Personnel management.
    3. Internationalists.   4. International trade.   5. International business enterprises—Employees—Training of.   I. Title.
HD2755.5.S33   1999   99-36069
658'.049—dc21   CIP

Cover design by Richard Ferguson
Text design by Sheryl Mehary

BookPartners, Inc.
P. O. Box 922
Wilsonville, Oregon 97071

*This book is dedicated to my husband, David—
who schlepped the bags*

Contents

Acknowledgments

It gives me great pleasure to acknowledge all the individuals I interviewed and to thank them for their time and consideration. The process was an education in the realities of international business ventures. Many of the following people are quoted and profiled in the book and in the endnotes, and to all I extend my gratitude for their insight and inspiration.

Kudos to my interpreters in Japan, Ukraine, and Hungary respectively: Ko Ajiki, Elena Vladimirova Lopato, and Adrienne Popovics. Without you, it would have been a complete mystery.

In addition, the following people have been exceptionally helpful with their research assistance and advice: Nancy Curren, Cathy Sunshine, Merrily Chafie, Deborah Hollands, Ruth Bleuzé, and Kathy Davis.

Gary Gomez deserves credit for designing and producing the models appearing in Chapters 1, 3, and 5.

For their support and belief in my project, thanks go to Dave Hopkins at University of Denver, Merrily Chafie, international business consultant, Bob Carrothers and Janet Fogarty of TEC Colorado, and my dear friends, Robin Blanc and Carolyn Byram.

A salute to my intrepid network, those people whose connections and introductions made the number of interviews possible and my visits to their countries and their contacts a joy. Satoshi Sato, Robert Liang, Zsolt Pozvai, Minh Le, Pedro Borio, Fernando Guntovitch, Austen Zecha, Patricia Fiske, John Lowe, Judith Pugh, Gloria Koshio, Mark Miller, Barbara Earley, Carol Hyatt, Sabrina Wilson, Dick and Gail West, and Tom Watkins.

And to my interviewees, my best thanks: Asma Abdullah, Exxon; Masayuki Arai, IB-Net; Bob Armstrong, Echo Bay Mines; Jack Barclay, Wire Rope Corp.; Jacques Bellmare, GTECH; Jason Blatt and Ye Ching, *The China Post;* Ruth Bleuzé, Prudential Intercultural Services; Larry Bosch, Celestial Seasonings; Leo Bryla, PASA Petroquímica; Tavia Campbell, US West International; Eduardo Caride, Telefónica de Argentina; Tapan Chakrabarty, CPC/AJI; Wayne Clark, Gates Rubber Company; Paul Codsi, PPG

Industries; Fernando Craverio, CH2M Hill; Elena DeMurias, Chemical/Chase Bank; Jiri Eibel, GTECH; Tom Fahey, Gates Rubber Company; Imre Felföldi, European Consulting Group; Patricia Fiske, Worldwide Partners; Glenn Haldeman, CH2M Hill; Stanislav Hemelík, Energoprojekt; Diane Holt, Central European Advisory Group; Jack Huang, The China Post; Soichi Ishijima, Pioneer Electronics; Glenn R. Jones, Jones International; Doug Kawahara, Becton-Dickinson; Pham Khai, OSC Vietnam; Bob King, Corporate Express; Gábor Kopiás, Kopiás Consulting; Don Lam, Deutsche Bank; Sonny Le, EniChem; Darlene Lee, Sofres FSA Taiwan; John Lowe, GTECH; Tina Ma, HR Consulting; Jock MacKenzie, Prosperity 2000; Margaret McLean, Holme, Roberts & Owen; Chris Murray, ABT Corporation; László Németh, Hungarian Development Foundation; Nguyen Xuan Oanh, NX Oanh Associates; Stewart Oldroyd, Oracle; Virginia Pían, Transcapital Group; Young Park, Young Park Associates; Victor Pavlenko, Russia Telecommunication Development Corp.; Jim Peters, Samsonite; Antonio-Carlos Rocha, GTECH; Tadao Sakakibara, Micron Machinery; Jairo Sanchez, Stafford-Miller; Javier Sato, PASA Petroquímica; Bob Stedman, Gates Rubber Company; Linda Sweeney, Kabelkom; Vladimir Tkachenko, Neptun; Wilson Tay, TEC International; Kevin Taylor, Snorkel; Johnny Tuan, Rock Records; Vo Van Hue, SoHa Farms; Susan Vonsild, Interlink; Elizabeth Wada, Melia Hotels; Titan Wang, SRT/AC Nielson; Jack Weidmaier, Wire Rope Corporation; Doug Williams, Chase Bank; Bill Wroblewski, Gates Rubber Company; Richard Wong, TEC International; Chow Chee Yan, TEC International.

Foreword:
Peeling the Onion

The subject of international business and its interaction with human relationships has fascinated me since my own expatriate experience, living and working for ten years in Europe. Wandering the world is a joy for me, so when I decided to write this book, I simultaneously decided that the only way to conduct authentic, realistic research for it was to ask the people who are directly involved in international ventures. This meant extensive travel — but that is no hardship to me.

I haven't always been a wanderer. When I was growing up in the American Midwest, my frame of reference extended just about around the block. My family rarely left the region, even for vacations. My first encounter with anything more exotic than Kansas City came when I traveled to Europe for the first time in the mid-1960s. Within three months, I was hooked on travel.

Several years later I had the good fortune to relocate to Europe for an extended period. It was only then that I felt the full impact of cultural difference. I had realized vaguely that things would not be the same, because I had the superficial impressions of a tourist, but I expected only to observe the differences rather than becoming intimately involved in them. It was a shock to discover how wrong this assumption was. I remember saying to a friend, "I don't ever remember feeling so *American!*" I wasn't saying this with a thrill of patriotism: I quite simply felt weird.

After a while, though, I adjusted and had a wonderful time. I could not have analyzed my experience at the time, but I now realize that I had slowly become a different person. My reactions to my new environment brought out characteristics and developed my talents in ways that allowed me to be successful internationally. At the time, I was working for an American college as regional director of educational programs on several military bases. I had to organize and staff fifteen geographically separate locations, recruit, hire, and train field staff, and travel extensively as a troubleshooter. Creativity and communication skills were a major part of my role: something was always awry somewhere, whether with American students, host-country nationals, foreign students, or expatriates.

When I moved back to the United States, I was confounded to encounter the same confusion and disorientation that I had experienced when I first went abroad. This sense of dislocation was even harder to deal with, because I didn't expect it. I had thought I was coming home. I didn't realize how profoundly my international experience had altered my cultural programming and changed my attitudes.

In addition, I didn't understand why my international decade was almost completely discounted by companies for which I wanted to work. They didn't understand what I had done "over there" and didn't seem to care, even though my achievements and understanding were intensely important to me. I now know that these skills *should* have been important to the U.S. companies as well.

Ever since that watershed period, I've been intrigued with cultural differences and fascinated by the unique nature, experiences, and struggles of the cosmopolites—the "citizens of the world"—with whom I felt an immediate affinity. As my business experience deepened, I simultaneously traveled more of the world on volunteer assignments, leisure travel, and visits to friends; I spent long periods in parts of the world that I had grown to love. I began to think more about the impact that business and culture have on each other, and how intensely they intertwine with the people who work in the world. I recognized that there were some interesting and unexplained issues related to the attitudes and practices of businesses operating internationally. I decided to find out what was behind this. My decision resulted in a research project that progressed through levels of understanding, much like peeling the proverbial onion; and, happily, it took me around the world.

I began my study by talking informally with some international business executives with whom I had become acquainted professionally. Just as I did, they knew that there was something unusual about people like us, but we could not quite define it. These discussions peeled away the first layer and led me to identify a distinct group—the people I am calling "internationalists."

Identifying what was different about "internationalists" led me to the next layer: the ways they are utilized organizationally and incorporated into their companies. Next came the project issues: what these people did "out there," and what happened as they did it. If they were successful, why did they succeed? And if they were not, why not?

As more layers fell away, I uncovered a central core or theme deep within them. That core is the uniqueness and the critical role of the internationalists, the people who act as business partners and unifying influences in tying projects throughout the world to the companies they serve.

Most of my research was done through face-to-face, audio-recorded interviews. I did not attempt to collect survey data; I wanted to hear personal stories. I asked only a few set questions and allowed people simply to talk about themselves, their companies, their projects, their frustrations, and their successes. I also wanted to hear about learning, feelings and opinions, so I asked them what they would have done differently, if anything. Finally, I asked what advice they would offer to companies as they spread their global wings. You will read their comments in their own words.

The concepts and suggestions my consultants offered are simply stated. But simple does not mean easy: it means uncomplicated. The practices of internationalists take patience, skill, and an extraordinary ability to deal with ambiguity. It requires a special person with a special type of mindset to be successful at this.

In finding ways to work successfully in the world, business-people should remember that harmony does not mean that everyone plays the same note. It is possible to create a remarkable whole from very different individual parts, and in doing so, to create an entity that is significantly greater than the sum of its components. When these many instruments are playing together, they can create a beautiful symphony.

I hope this book is a useful tool for companies and people working across the world's borders. It is intended as a resource for corporate leaders, human resources leaders, internationalists, and those who are studying or otherwise preparing for international careers. May peeling the layers of this subject be as fascinating for you as it has been for me.

1

Themes, Strategies, and the Internationalist

During the research for this book, I had the pleasure of meeting and interviewing sixty-five international business executives, managers, and project leaders, as well as several wise and experienced retired international executives, on four continents. All of them were directly involved in international business ventures. I also talked informally and endlessly with many others I met during my travels.

The interviews covered a very wide range of industries: banking and finance, oil and gas, mining, petrochemicals, manufacturing, gaming, publishing, travel and tourism, telecommunications and media, government, energy, high technology, foods and beverages, biotechnology, wholesale and distribution, and a host of professional services. Offering their views were fifty men and fifteen women; forty-one of them were executives, seventeen were in management, and seven were consulting professionals. To conduct these interviews I traveled around the globe, visiting North America (27 interviews), Asia (19), Latin America (7), and Western, Central, and Eastern Europe (12). The companies ranged in size from small professional firms to multinational corporations employing thousands. At the same time, I read widely on all aspects of international business. I came away with a fascinating education in the realities of this sphere.

People talked to me about projects of all sizes: some lasted a few months, while others extended over many years. Among the structures we discussed were wholly owned subsidiaries, joint ventures, privatizations, equity investments, and strategic alliances.

This broad sampling was deliberate. I didn't set out to assess the quality or viability of business schemes or financing solutions. Instead, I wanted to hear personal stories about what people actually did out there—about their successes, frustrations, and challenges. Even more, I wanted to hear what they had learned in hindsight and to reap their advice for others in the international game. Often themes surfaced that seemed to be common to such projects, regardless of their size, type, industry, or geography.

Common Themes

Following are the prevailing themes drawn from my research and interviews about people's experiences starting and building businesses on four continents. Although these businesspeople expressed their successes and frustrations in different ways, they clearly identified certain crucial concerns. Some of these issues are organizational, and others arise at the project level.

Top-level corporate support from the CEO, the management team, and the board of directors is absolutely essential.

Several executives I interviewed recommended that a corporation going international should start small. Carefully select the proposed projects that have the best chance of success. Choose a location with care, staff the field site extremely well, and leave plenty of room for adaptation. Keep the corporate leadership focused on these few critical projects.

Many international project leaders expressed frustration because of their inability to get the attention of their corporate leaders. They thought that being out of immediate view led their projects to fade from the corporation's collective consciousness. They felt sidelined and trivialized; they complained their needs and requests were met with impatience, like those of bothersome children. People who had this experience felt personally abandoned or ignored. (Chapters 2 and 5 offer strategies and tactics to overcome these problems.)

Each market is different and brings its own set of challenges. Success comes from learning the significant features of a new market and culture when there is enough flexibility to adjust, as well as enough money and energy to provide adequate resources. Thus, it is of paramount importance to select a manageable number of projects that can command the attention and focus of the organization's leaders.

International projects usually take longer to show results and cost more than organizations anticipate.

Changing politics, fluctuating economic conditions, unpredictable exchange rates, poor selection of international partners, and complications among project team members were among the reasons often cited for slow development and high costs. Some of these contingencies are inevitable risks of going international, some can be foreseen and avoided. I often heard the lament, "We knew we would encounter cultural differences, but we didn't understand the depth or breadth of those differences, or how they would affect our business goals."

An issue that was noted repeatedly was the difficulties project teams had in getting started and maintaining a pace. Executives and team leaders talked about the challenges of forming a cohesive multicultural work group. They mentioned inability to reach decisions, differing senses of urgency among team members, and failure to understand roles. Of course, the longer it took to form a functioning team, the more costs rose. Sometimes project leaders recognized that these differences were culturally inspired, but they had rarely anticipated them.

In hindsight, project leaders determinedly stressed the need for appropriate leadership and team development at the outset, and for continuing team support throughout the life of the project. Human nature will always inject itself into, and frequently delay, business plans, and the expression of human nature is always filtered through culture. Selecting a project leader who understands and responds to this fact is an important first step in achieving success.

Clashing corporate cultures can become a significant barrier to success.

During the interviews, I was struck by the effect of organizational culture and the number of times that it was mentioned as a major challenge. Organizations have distinct cultures, influenced by the culture in which they originate. Their culture is also influenced by leadership style, structure, and staffing—all products of where that company originates. Further, individual companies or categories of business often have their own versions of their culture's work practices. Social scientists call such self-identified, self-chosen cultural entities "communities of practice." A huge multinational corporation such as IBM may have a distinct culture worldwide. Government employees, bankers, or oil explorers may constitute separate communities of practice, each a little more distinct within its own distinct national culture.

These overlapping cultures and subcultures are difficult to anticipate or define. In the sample I studied, for instance, business ventures between private and public companies were seen to pose exceptionally difficult challenges. Except within huge multinationals, differences in corporate culture regularly caused difficulties in group dynamics.

Astute international executives and managers, particularly those who were currently leading projects, placed great emphasis on this point. They spoke strongly about the need to recognize distinct organizational differences from the outset and to implement team development processes to overcome them. They also remarked that forging cohesiveness was an ongoing process, and that they spent as much time on this as they did on the other aspects of their projects. (Chapters 3 and 5 treat this topic in more detail.)

Lack of common vision is a fundamental problem at the project level.

After a series of meetings in which the word "vision" was used frequently, it became clear to me that many struggles occurred because multicultural work groups weren't quite sure what their collective goals were. The more organizations, team members, and interests involved, the muddier the goals became, and the more fractured the focus.

The people I interviewed almost universally addressed the issue of common vision as the single most critical aspect of business performance. Many had begun their projects assuming that everyone involved shared the same goal, so they spent little or no time making sure they were all on the same path. Too often, however, the activities of individuals from different organizations were directed toward political positioning within their own organizations and furthering their own interests rather than those of the partnership. Businesspeople from different nations (including the United States) asserted that this was particularly true of personnel from Western companies. Chow Chee Yan, an astute Malaysian businessman with whom I spent a fascinating hour in Kuala Lumpur, summed it up succinctly by quoting a Chinese proverb: "Just because you sleep in the same bed doesn't mean you have the same dream."[1]

Good project leadership is critical to success.

International project leaders report that they spend as much time developing and maintaining team unity as they do on "hard" business activities. This interpersonal, intercultural task requires patience, flexibility, and sensitivity to differences. Nevertheless, many of the leaders I interviewed, and others we discussed, appear to have been selected for their technical skills alone. Leaders and other team members may have been chosen simply because they were available, because they agreed to relocate, because it was their "turn," or on some other criterion of simple expediency. This appeared to happen much more commonly in Western companies; in

Asian companies, by contrast, leadership qualities and personality characteristics were strong factors in selection. Western companies only occasionally considered the attitudes, behaviors, or mindset in selecting potential project leaders. Yet when the projects were actually operational, it was mindset that ultimately proved to be the factor most critical to the success of the group. Attitudes and characteristics were just as important as technical capabilities when project leaders found themselves spending as much time developing team relationships as conducting the "business of the business."

Again and again my consultants mentioned attitudes that were critical to success in international ventures. Concepts that came up frequently were flexibility, adaptability, curiosity, and the ability to deal with ambiguity. Stephen K. Rhinesmith does a good job of describing the successful "mindset": "People with a global mindset look at the world as an arena in which to express their talents, maximize their success, and influence others. The global mind sees the world as a playground as well a school."[2]

Companies have constant problems finding people who will accept an international assignment.

This challenge was mentioned regularly, and it appears to have two roots. First, many corporations do not understand that they need people with unique attitudes and attributes to work internationally. Second, even organizations that do know this usually have a difficult time finding and keeping professionals who plan and pursue careers in international business. Solving these problems is a big job. It requires what Danah Zohar calls "rewiring the corporate brain."[3]

This rethinking begins with *broadening the concept of who is valuable*. Western companies have a collective consciousness that places high value on technical competence, professional achievements, and measured results. Those are the people who are rewarded, recognized, and promoted—the people who have clear career potential. Even though personal characteristics and attitudes might be said to be important, they are usually secondary factors in international staffing decisions.

This is the very foundation of the frustration expressed by the many executives who say they can't find anyone who wants to move onto the international playing field. Why would people want to go abroad, when little or no value is placed on the very qualities that would make them successful? Talented staff members have observed the well-documented and widespread disaffection of returned expatriates—their dislocation and inability to "come home." Ambitious engineers, MBAs, or technical professionals may well be unwilling to put their careers on the line by risking an assignment that would remove them from the place where their skills and abilities are valued and where they have access to corporate-political power. They are aware that plunging into a foreign environment may alienate them from the sources of power and force them to develop behaviors that may be distinctly different from those with which they are comfortable.

A New Profession for a New Century

Some corporate leaders seemed quite surprised when, in conversations or in presentations, I introduced the concept of a unique internationalist mindset. This reaction was much more common in the United States than in Europe, where internationalism has long been a way of life; many Europeans grow up multilingual and cross national borders regularly. In Asia the concept is not only understood but indeed highly valued.

When corporations aren't sure who these people *are,* then they are unlikely to know how to find, recruit, develop, and hold onto them. Furthermore, there appears to be no real niche for them in many businesses. Corporations that have not yet recognized what makes a person successful internationally will not have created roles or career paths to nurture the international people they need.

The other side of this challenge confronts the people who have been tapped to "go international." Frequently they seem to have become internationalized by default, having been plucked from their corporate roles because of their technical knowledge, seniority, or willingness, or as a result of corporate politics. Some people selected this way do well in their new roles and discover something important about themselves and their place in the scheme of things. Others, however, fail disastrously. Moreover, even those who succeed may have trouble returning to the corporate family with ease and may complain that the company doesn't understand them any more—while the home staff claim that the repatriates have been out of touch and don't understand *them*. In situations like these, everyone loses.

Because so many of the people I interviewed talked about the uniqueness of successful international people in a hazy, undefined way, it became clear that a definition was needed. The fact that none existed was telling. A host of problems arose from the simple fact that since there was no way to describe what kind of person succeeds in the international arena, there was no way to identify the individuals who were likely to succeed.

There are certain spirits who plunge into new environments and take with them the ability to create a successful business experience in strange and confusing surroundings. These people come out of a corporate home equipped with the organizational culture and mission, and launch into the international scene to grapple with logistics and cultural issues. The ones who make it have a set of unique characteristics that enable them to make this quantum jump from inside to outside, taking along their knowledge, assumptions, and behaviors as well as their assigned tasks. They can create or manage a business situation in ambiguous circumstances—situations where they cannot identify black-and-white rules. They can unlearn what they know and create new understandings and systems. And they can move on easily when their part of the project is completed.

The following definition of a successful international person, an "internationalist," is a composite of answers from many people I asked about these qualities. It identifies what I have come to believe is a new global profession which is exceedingly and increasingly important. Considering the internationalist as a new breed of professional has profound implications for the ways corporations find and manage their precious human capital. It also has profound implications for individuals considering their careers, and for academic institutions that prepare people for international careers.

The Internationalist

The internationalist is one who lives and works or travels regularly to work outside his or her country of origin, or outside the country where a primary business is located, and who regularly interacts with business associates from other countries. This person possesses professional competence coupled with a global mindset characterized by tolerance, flexibility, curiosity, and the ability to deal with ambiguity.

As I interviewed more and more corporate executives who expressed confusion and frustration when asked to characterize people who they thought were good choices for international work, I began to consider the corporate environments, fed by educational institutions that were in turn supported by social and political environments; there were many points at which confusion could arise. Danah Zohar characterizes the cultures of organizations as "Newtonian" (Western) or "Networked" (Eastern).[4] These organizations are products of the culture in which they grew, as are the people who work in them. In a Newtonian or Western culture, value is placed on individualism, mechanics, immutable laws, science and its dictates. The Networked or Eastern organization is based on relationships and values, consensus and negotiated results.

The significant differences in corporate mindset became clearer every time the subject of strategy arose. I heard a great deal from Western executives about emerging markets, opportunities, competitive edge, focus, quality, and service. I realized that many companies have a mechanistic attitude about their businesses and concentrate on market potential, finance, bottom-line results, and the legal complexities of doing business in other parts of the world. When I was interviewing Asian executives, however, the strategy question elicited responses that included such elements as careful selection of location and partners and the appropriate choice of expatriates. These two points were frequently missing from Western responses. The Eastern executives were significantly more aware of what it took to be successful internationally, and they quickly made it clear that this was a major part of their selection process.

This is not to say that Eastern is superior to Western, or that all Western organizations are doing a poor job in international staffing. Many large multinationals know no boundaries and have well-developed plans and processes for finding international talent. What is important is that *all* globalizing organizations define the internationalist clearly and recognize the value of *characteristics* as well as the technical competencies that are currently the basis for most international staffing decisions in Western companies.

Looking for internationalists within an organization is cutting across functional lines in a different way. Organizations typically have pools of talent in the executive, finance, operations, marketing, and sales functions. Looking for talented internationalists should cut vertically through each function, as shown in the table on the next page.

A Strategic Blueprint

Identifying and writing down this list of common challenges is useful in that it condenses myriad situations to a manageable size. Finding solutions is not so simple. A solution implies a one-size-fits-all approach—something done after a problem arises. A strategic approach makes more sense, because it can be applied in the planning and anticipation process. So, after I had asked my interviewees about their challenges, I asked for their thoughts on strategies to prevent or overcome these challenges. Here are their ideas, followed by Table 2 showing where the common challenges and recommended strategies mesh.

Functional Expertise

Internationalist Traits

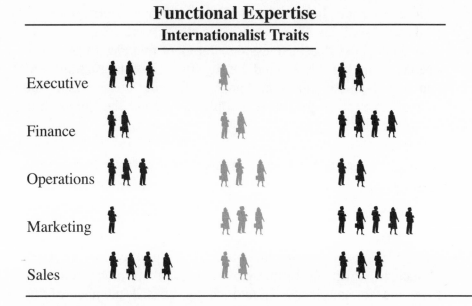

Executive			
Finance			
Operations			
Marketing			
Sales			

Table 1. *Recruiters can look in each department of a company to find the people who have internationalist characteristics.*

Link the corporate visions, goals, and strategic plan to human resources needs.

Work at broadening the corporate perception of which employees are valuable and promotable. Plan for internationalization with recruitment, training, leadership development, and career paths that internally recognize and promote people with skills and interests in the international arena. Analyze the corporate strategic plan, linking human resources needs to it, and focus on finding talent from around the world or selected geographic areas of planned expansion.

Look for young creative thinkers in areas of study other than business and technology: philosophy, social sciences, history, or music. Hire some of these potential internationalists at entry level, then provide adequate training to teach them the "business of the business" from inside, in a development program that trains them in both the appropriate technology and the corporate culture, vision, and goals. In other words, grow your own internationalists. (This will be discussed in detail in chapter 2.)

Make sure that business development teams who go out to open new markets understand the significance of internationalists, and that their strategic plans provide for the identification and recruitment of appropriate people to bring the plans into existence.

Carefully select and develop a trusted local partner. Trust and relationships are the bedrock of successful business nearly everywhere.

A local business or mentor relationship is a powerful way to gain an intimate understanding of the social, political, and business climate in which the business venture is taking place. Someone from the foreign locale should be an official member of the business team, or a trusted unofficial advisor. He or she should be available to steer foreign partners through the often confusing, convoluted, and mostly unwritten rules of appropriate contacts and political and bureaucratic connections.

Glenn Haldeman, vice president and general manager of CH2M Hill's Latin American operations, emphasizes this: "Make sure you have good, strong local technical and political partners. Then, some [headquarters] person needs to take ownership, to live and breathe it and don't do it long distance."[5] This advice was corroborated by many people I interviewed.

In most of the world, trust and relationships are primary business tools. Many businesspeople outside the United States are completely confounded by the Western practice of *not* doing business with one's friends.

Many countries require some percentage of local ownership before they will permit foreign investment or business presence in the country. Even where such requirements are nonexistent or unenforced, however, a trusted local partner with an intimate understanding of the local explicit and implicit rules of business will be able to navigate the bureaucratic and cultural waters much more effectively than a foreigner can.

Support international ventures with enough attention and appropriate resources to get them going.

"Resources" include both capital requirements and human beings. This means staffing to manage the project, people in the field to support it, and people at the corporate home to provide coordination and liaison. Identifying the right human capital deserves as much attention as financial analysis and logistic planning. The selection process should take into account the internationalist characteristics of flexibility, adaptability, curiosity, and willingness, along with the appropriate technical and business capabilities and experience.

Choosing the right person for a particular stage of the business is also critical. Several executives who had spent years in the international arena spoke about the need for more youthful and energetic assignees. They contend that an international assignment is not for the faint-hearted nor for the businessperson who is firmly established in a pattern of behavior and management style. Because culture, values and style play such an important part in business ventures, they argue, someone who has the energy, flexibility, and tolerance to deal with continuous uncertainty and change is necessary. Other executives, however, believed just as strongly that it is foolhardy to send out someone who lacks the maturity and balance of the seasoned manager. Although this may seem to be a division of opinion, the answers are not so disparate if one considers the different needs that are associated with different developmental stages of a venture.

Initially, in small start-up operations, management needs follow the size of the organization. A new venture in a new market begs for energy, creativity, and an entrepreneurial spirit—someone who is comfortable with risk and has a high tolerance for rapid change. As the business venture and market mature, a different kind of internationalist is called for: one with more seasoning and management sophistication.

International projects require the creation of a new culture that
is a blend of many parts and greater than their sum.

When businesses blend, as in a joint venture or strategic
alliance, different organizational practices can clash. When people
from more than one culture work together, differences in expectations, work practices, values, and behaviors create stress. Cumula-
tive clashes can really bring about chaos.

The goal of a multicultural work group, or team, is to create a
new culture that is a blend, both organizationally and culturally, of
its parts. *Flexibility* and *adaptation* are the operative words. In the
case of a multinational corporation, the headquarters may intend to
export its culture around the world. In doing so, it should export the
best of its practices, processes, and systems, but it should also adapt
to local business customs and values. In the case of a completely
new organization formed as a venture between other organizations,
the goal is more likely to be the creation of something completely
new that participants can claim as their own: that is, their self-
defined community of practice. (See chapter 5, "Internationalization
Solutions.") In doing so, they build a unit with the potential to be
more powerful and inventive than any of its individual components.

Give internationalists the tools they need to succeed, and then
let them use them.

An international assignment is like no other. Organizations
wouldn't send someone into a critical business situation unprepared, without the information or tools needed to handle delicate
negotiations or make appropriate decisions that could affect service
or production. International venturers should be equally well
chosen and well prepared, with cultural training, support systems,
team-building skills, and the necessary long-term career planning
to send them out and bring them back successfully.

Project managers and executives abroad should have a direct
pipeline back to their corporate home, with someone on the other
end who will listen and respond appropriately. They also need the
autonomy to run their own show as they learn from experience. In

several interviews, internationalists expressed ongoing frustration with corporate interference by people who did not understand the day-to-day challenges or circumstances of the project, and who were not available to help or provide regular guidance. People in the field need to make sure that corporate leaders really know and understand the foreign venture. (See chapter 5, "Internationalization Solutions.")

In Argentina I met a talented and skilled international executive, Eduardo Caride, who commented:

> *When you are a project leader, you always have persons that have opinions of the transactions that are not involved in them. They are always, I like to say — they enter the subject through the windows. Just have a quick look around and make a decision. This is what troubles transactions. You work with a team, then you have to go back to your constituencies and try to support or to defend the deal you are working on and everybody comes and has opinions, with their own personal issues. It causes a lot of fights.*[6]

Expect the unexpected. Plan for it.

Take logistics and cultural issues into account when establishing timing and budget guidelines; stay flexible; and don't quit too soon. Projects can be effectively stalled by very simple things. For instance, in emerging markets where basic services are erratic, reliable electric power can be an issue. I heard stories about old office buildings where inadequate wiring caused fires in new offices. Forces of nature, like typhoons and floods, can stop production and shipment of goods. Telephone service is a challenge when only two unreliable lines are available in an office to support fifteen people. In some countries, outbreaks of disease, religious controversy, or civil unrest have delayed business activities.

These are only a few of the actual unexpected, unplanned logistical problems related by interviewees. No specific situations can be anticipated, but some kinds of problems *should* be expected. Markets should be studied thoroughly in advance with the anticipation that delays and inconveniences will occur, particularly in developing countries.

Anticipate cultural issues and expect them to arise—because they will. Always. Forcing project timelines causes endless difficulties. Few places in the world place as much emphasis on time as the United States and northern Europe. To much of the rest of the world, time is a commodity to be stretched. When timelines are exceeded, budgets usually are too. And when budgets run over, companies usually want to stop the bleeding. In international ventures, it's important to utilize longer-term thinking and to assess the probabilities of success down the road. If budgets are prepared with some flexibility and renegotiation built in, there is a better chance for success than if everything is written in stone.

The director of international staffing for a multinational high-tech company,[7] an experienced internationalist, suggested that project planners ask themselves a series of questions before embarking on a new venture. These are directly related to the fact that international project timelines are regularly exceeded:

- What is our expected time for return on investment?
- If we did the same project (at home), how would we do it?
- Are there any differences? What and why?

He then suggested that companies take the time frame that looked most outrageous to them, and double it. Most of the interviewees agreed.

Seek out — and listen to — the voices of experience.

No teacher or book can provide the depth of understanding that we can gain from first-hand experience. When going into a new market, ask people who have been there. Talk to businessmen and women already in place and succeeding in your potential market. Find out about local pitfalls, attitudes, behaviors, and expectations. Ask about their challenges and seek their advice.

Take advantage of your own in-house talent. Several interviewees expressed regret that they hadn't sought the advice of former

Table 2. Challenges and Strategies: How they Relate. The topics discussed in this chapter intersect as shown.

Challenges	Strategies						
	Link corporate strategic plan to HR needs	Select trusted local partner	Support int'l ventures with attention and resources	Int'l projects require creation of new, blended culture	Give internationalists tools and let them succeed	Expect the unexpected	Listen to experience
Top level support essential	X	X	X		X	X	X
Int'l projects take longer than planned and cost more		X	X			X	X
Clashing corporate cultures a barrier to success		X		X	X	X	X
Lack of common vision a problem at project level		X		X			X
Good project leadership essential	X			X			X
Companies have problems finding people who will accept int'l assignment	X		X				X

expatriates or internationalists, now retired or moved on. These are people with a wealth of accumulated information that may have little to do with the technicalities of your particular business venture, but everything to do with the very human aspects of functioning in a different world.

Gaskets and Seals

As these themes became clearer, they fell logically into groups representing organizational, project, and individual components. Typically, ventures progressed well as planning and analysis went on at a corporate or organizational level, but as implementation got close, things became more challenging.

What changed as a project moved from one level to another? Operational management was taken out of a controlled location and moved into one that was variable, if not indeed volatile.

And who did the moving? People did: the general managers, the financial managers, and the professionals—the project leaders. It was those selected to manage the international project who took the plans into the field and either made them work or not. They were the ones who had to deal with the vagaries of foreign locales and adjust themselves and the company's plans. But at the critical point of moving to the field, projects were often staffed and led by people who were chosen simply out of expediency.

The group of "organizational" issues described to me had to do primarily with planning, logistics, and finding the right people. The "project" issues centered around leadership, organizational support, team development, local relationships, and logistics. During the analyses that followed these fascinating meetings, I found that the problems encountered by each side—organizational and project—could be linked in the middle. What created the mesh of the two areas was the people selected by the organization to carry out the plans in the international arena.

Figure 1 illustrates the role of the internationalist in graphic and metaphorical form. The two parts of the project are the organizational level of project conception (usually a fairly tidy or at least

Figure 1. *International ventures begin at the organization level, first with planning and procedures and then with people to implement the plan and carry it to the field. In between is the critical internationalist, who acts as the "gasket" to connect the two. The gasket is flexible, able to deal with unexpected rough spots, and it provides the seal between the organization and the field.*

predictable process) and the implementation level in the field (which rarely is tidy or predictable). Between them comes the internationalist, who acts as the "gasket" in the middle. That gasket is the critical central part that holds the two stages together, providing a flexible seal between the relatively well-defined plans of the organization level and the unpredictability of the field. Insert the wrong gasket in a machine, and the two sides won't seal. Everyone knows what happens when a gasket fails: things leak, and the gasket has to be replaced—an operation that invariably costs the project both time and money.

The figure presents the significance of the internationalist operating as that indispensable gasket. In the final analysis, it is always carefully chosen, skilled people who make the business strategy work.

Summary

Several universal problem areas emerged during interviews and discussions with many internationalists and executives on four continents. These problems were expressed in terms of organizational, project, and human dimensions.

Much time, money and energy are wasted during international projects. Successes certainly occur, but frequently at a much higher cost than originally anticipated. Often, the reasons that companies do not achieve their goals stem more from the difficulties of making the *people* functional than from any inherent weakness in the business planning.

Corporations, particularly Western ones, have a mindset based in science and technology. They value and seek employees with specific business skills and training. They typically do not evaluate potential employees based on the fundamental internationalist characteristics of flexibility, adaptability, curiosity, and ability to deal with ambiguity. Yet these are the very people who are successful internationally. When Western corporations want people to accept international assignments, they have to look for those who possess these characteristics along with the technical abilities they frequently seek almost exclusively.

Not paying attention to human and organizational differences slows things down and causes a great deal of expensive trouble. Anticipating this, recruiting the right people, planning carefully, providing cultural and team development training ideally in advance of a project, can prevent many problems.

Internationalists play a vital role in the success of cross-border business projects. Planning strategically for international ventures and linking that strategy to human resources needs is absolutely necessary for companies that expect to succeed and be competitive internationally.

2

The 30,000-Foot (or 9,000-Meter) View: Organizations and the Internationalist

Today the United States is a driving force in the world economic equation. The country's powerful business engine has been built by an astoundingly mixed population. In little more than two centuries the nation has grown into a global powerhouse. As in all culturally mixed nations, growth and cohesiveness have sometimes been threatened as the country grappled with ethnic differences and the slow evolution toward a uniquely American culture. This deliberate and unprecedented demographic diversity has produced a creative, spirited, energetic populace marked by a will to succeed. The American melting pot attracted risk-takers from many lands with promises of opportunity. They came and they created and they succeeded.

We can draw a parallel with companies in the international arena. It's not a difficult step to assume that powerful diversity like that in North America can and will produce phenomenal results, given the right mix of environment and leadership. These are major advantages that can be translated into the international arena. If corporations are willing and able to address some human issues, they can become even stronger as they globalize.

Corporate Mindset

Companies that have never before been in competition because of geographic separation are today meeting in head-on market challenges as a result of globalization. As this trend escalates, it's increasingly clear that what really differentiates companies is their people. Virtually everything else can be either copied or bought. The need for internationalist talent has never been clearer or more critical, but—and here is the crux—all too few companies know it. Or, if they say they know it, they fail to design systems and implement practices to bring these people in, keep them, and use them effectively.

This chapter is concerned with strategic planning and systems for internationalizing organizations. Many of these have no strategic plan or system for their essential international resource: human capital. In a recent study conducted by Harvard Business School in conjunction with AMROP International, nearly a thousand CEOs and international executives in more than thirty countries responded clearly: "For 'global management' to become a reality for more organizations, it is critical that the CEOs in those organizations get more involved." [1]

The study found that only 38 percent of respondents indicated that their CEO formulated objectives, strategies, and tactics relating to the careers of international executives; nonetheless, almost twice as many respondents believed that such input will be critical to the process in the future. The study also found that those companies whose CEOs are actively involved report greater success internationally than those who are not. This finding definitively supports the points my interviewees made, as reported in chapter 1. A major issue, they said, was a need for the involvement and support of corporate leadership.

During my research, I was amazed by the lack of written material that addressed corporate strategy for acquiring, keeping, and effectively using international talent. Articles about staffing appear to be directed largely toward assuring compliance with employment laws, with an outlook purely on the present. This attitude is a direct reflection of a Western corporate mindset which has become progressively more mechanistic and technical. The current trend toward greater focus on numbers and weaker focus on people exacerbates this problem.

If companies are unaware that they need internationalists, they obviously won't have the internal systems to recruit, select, train, develop, or retain them. Solving this problem requires a change in corporate thinking: a recognition of the value of internationalists and the unique qualities they bring.

From this discussion, it seems clear:

Strategic planning, which includes internationalization, must be linked to human resources planning so that talent is on hand to carry out planned expansion.

As a company matures in the international arena, it's increasingly important that its senior management team, including the board of directors, be neither monoracial nor monocultural. It should also include people who have had international experience and can appreciate the value and perspective that such diversity brings. Respondents in many countries clearly said that only people who have actually *been* internationalists really understand the complexities of global business. Those who haven't, don't. It's not something you can learn in school.

People working internationally have a lot to deal with besides the business of the business. And, they hastened to add, international experience did not mean a first-class airplane trip to Paris, with a view of the city skyline from the top floor of the Hotel George V. Work in the trenches counts, and if leadership roles in an internationalizing company are filled by people who have never been outside their own country except to vacation, trouble can be expected.

Using a long-term strategy, companies can build a multinational employee base within their organizations, accomplishing the need to diversify and develop their own international talent in house. Over a period of years, internationalist employees from various parts of the world can gain the experience and seasoning to take their places at the top.

I met Susan Vonsild, an astute Danish consultant who works internationally. She said:

> *We're talking about organizational change. It has to start at the top, and that might take some time if you have companies with traditional leadership. Then you have to wait until that generation is away and get the next generation in who have had foreign assignments. Or get someone on the board of directors who comes from a different country or represents international experience in some way. So those (international) success criteria get put more and more in place until you have to have international experience to progress in the organization. Then you start building in programs for younger people where you have them on rotating, short assignments in another country. Get into mentor relationships. Bring them back, then build up a base in the organization. Then your internationalists can be someone with that experience. If you're just putting one token person with international experience in the organization, it won't work. It has to spread throughout.[2]*

Creating a Place

An organizational issue of concern to both executives and internationalists had to do with internal systems to support international people. They identified the need for an internal career development system that allows for identification of international opportunities, training, coaching and mobility, and succession planning. The Harvard-AMROP study found that "two key strategies are linked to success: reliance on centralized personnel policies for the development of (international) executives and the establishment of a formal succession and development program." The writers of this study also found that few are actually using these programs; they likened the current conditions to "survival of the fittest." In direct support of my interviewees' comments, they write that North American corporate respondents placed lower emphasis on language studies and international management courses than did respondents from the rest of the world.[3]

From analysis of the interviewee responses and many conversations with management consultants experienced in organizational design, I drew four groups of questions that can be used to examine where a company is now and what needs to change so that an internal framework can be implemented to support internationalists.

1. *Is there an awareness in the company of what it means to be a global corporation?* Is it acknowledged and supported at the top and throughout the organization?

2. *Is the role of the internationalist defined?* Do they exist in the company? Do people in the company know what the role is all about, what attitudes and attributes are characteristic of internationalists, and what it takes to be one? Are internationalists important and recognized?

3. *Is there an active effort to find and identify internationalists internally and externally?* Does the company seek talent from sources other than well-known graduate programs? From schools with international degree programs? From the Peace Corps or other international volunteer organizations? From foreign schools? From informal internal systems in which managers, both domestic and international, are encouraged to recognize, recommend and mentor talent they identify?

4. *Are there internal systems to support the role of internationalist?* Are internationalists hired, developed and trained specifically for international roles? Is there a system in place to move them around as needed or for training? Can they be sent out, moved around, and brought back successfully? Is their experience important and valued? Are they heard? Is there a career path structure in place that will support them?

The Internationalists

In asking these questions, it's not hard to see that establishing career systems for internationalists poses an interesting dilemma. You can't design a system specifically for internationalists if you don't have one that works for the rest of the organization. Internationalist careers will have to be viewed within the larger context of the whole system. The old process of career ladders and levels with associated increases in responsibility and compensation will likely not work in an organization that perceives itself as global. With mounting realization of the need for internationalists, and with increasing emphasis on characteristics and attitudes, style and intuition, understanding grows that the old mechanical practices need revision. They need to be replaced by flexible and creative ways that individuals can visualize and manage their own careers throughout the entire organization.

It isn't feasible to describe more than generically how such a system should work. Each one will and should be designed to fit a specific organization, industry, location, and corporate culture. That is the realm of the HR strategic planners who work with top management to link the corporate business goals with human resources strategy. It will also probably be customized for different business or operating units. However, it is possible to identify certain elements that should always be in place, no matter what variables dictate the specific design. These elements include:

- Corporate culture and leadership attitudes that encourage creativity, learning, and employee development, and that welcome change.
- Organizational communication processes to disseminate corporate values, strategy, and skills for the future needs of the business.
- Career development training for employees to encourage responsibility and provide methods for career planning. Concurrent training for supervisors as partners to coach, help set goals, and plan.
- Internal opportunity postings that are accessible to everyone, everywhere, and that are accompanied by development aids and guides.

- Analysis and descriptions of positions detailing behaviors, attitudes, and attributes as well as skills and experience.
- Availability of rotational assignments between divisions, with emphasis on development and training in functional areas.
- Availability of career advisors and mentors.
- Training opportunities that are available to encourage interest in new fields as well as to upgrade skills for current positions or advancement.
- Assessments for attitudes and attributes as well as skills.

This career planning and developmental methodology, of course, depends on the existence of organizational values and structures to support it, and on companies that believe in and actively recruit and develop those who plan international careers. Here we come back again to the bedrock issues: the corporate mindset and the attitudes about which employees are of most value.

Smaller companies that are just starting to "go global" might feel that they are too small for a complex internal career path or development system. They should still be aware of the internationalist characteristics and take care to select their expatriates internally or seek them outside the organization. International expansion is too important to a growing organization to risk sending out anyone but a person who has these special characteristics and training, coupled with the appropriate technical and professional skills.

The following sections of this chapter are a compilation of the wisdom of many people from various parts of the world. They talked about how it is and how it should be, with regard to internationalizing the "people" aspects of business: recruitment, selection, development, expatriation, inpatriation (bringing foreign nationals into a company from outside the country), and repatriation. Much of what they said was supported by empirical evidence from studies cited throughout this chapter.

Recruiting Internationalists

Tom Fahey, a retired international executive, told me:

> *I've lived overseas more than half of my adult life and the people I have met in international business—a good 90 percent of those who are out there doing international business, never did international studies, never studied languages, have no liberal arts background. They get sent out because they have some specific skill within their company. There are some exceptions, but that is not the standard. I do some work now for (intercultural training companies) and the great majority of people that come through there, in my experience, are almost always engineers or have a technical background. There is nothing in their background that prepares them for international business.[4]*

US News and World Report recently published a feature titled "America's Best Graduate Schools," reporting its exclusive rankings for 1998.[5] The five major fields of study identified are business, law, medicine, education, and engineering, followed by the fields of health and public affairs. Data are presented to compare the schools' strengths. Nowhere is there any mention of international studies as a major discipline; it is assigned to the category of "specialty."

In the *Denver Post* of May 8, 1998, an Associated Press article by Cliff Edwards cited a study by the University of Michigan that showed that the graduates with the highest starting salaries were in engineering specialties and computer science.[6] Liberal arts graduates are in the bottom five. This survey shows that salaries for engineers had risen 4 to 5 percent and now start around $40,000, while liberal arts graduates start around $25,000, representing an increase of around 2 percent.

Fahey's observations and the articles are graphic reflections of who Western corporations value and who is deemed worthy of attention in the fierce competition to recruit top graduates. I heard repeatedly from my Western interviewees that recruitment and selection, both at entry level and for positions within companies, was based mainly on technical criteria. Several colleagues and friends who are in the executive recruiting business talked about the people they "head-hunt." In nearly all cases, these are technical specialists, engineers, financial experts, or industry specialists. In fact, they can't keep up with the unending corporate demand.

These people are inarguably valuable and vital to growing and expanding organizations. But that is not the whole story. A company that perceives itself as global also needs people who possess the vital internationalist characteristics. When corporations begin to recognize that they need internationalist talent to sustain and expand their worldwide business activities, they will simultaneously expand their understanding of who is valuable to them.

The identification dilemma

Many corporate executives with whom I spoke talked about their difficulties identifying people they felt would accept and succeed in international assignments. If that is true, then perhaps part of the problem originates with their entry-level hiring choices. Developing people to meet the needs of international business should be a long-term, ongoing process—growing your own internationalists. Growing your own presupposes that you begin recruiting at entry level and develop that young base in their career paths. It was suggested by some experienced internationalists that corporations hire "internationally focused" people in addition to recruiting the traditional business administration, technical, and marketing talent. In other words, balance business knowledge with international capabilities. It was even suggested that as many as one-third of potential management new-hires possess the ability to become internationalists.

I asked the question, "How do you know if a person is internationally focused?" Most Western companies are accustomed to basing hiring decisions on quantifiable skills, technical and

The Internationalists

professional experience, and education. These criteria are easily identifiable and measurable. Finding someone with a quality as nebulous as "international focus" is quite another story.

There was a host of ideas about how such people can be identified. A prominent suggestion was, naturally, to look for people who already had international experience. Additional criteria included the following:

- Overseas military experience
- A college year abroad
- Peace Corps or other international volunteer work
- Being an immigrant
- Spending time with relatives in other countries
- Taking a year off to travel the world
- Having foreign-born parents who spoke two or more languages
- Degrees in international studies or languages

Tom Fahey told me:

Universities churn out a lot of people who think they want to be international. The thing I looked for in interviewing was what I call "vocation." They have to prove to me that they REALLY want it. Did they build houses for a summer in Costa Rica? Did they go live with a family or hitchhike for a year through Europe? They have to have actually done it. You have to have a real love for this different kind of life and a willingness to leave family and friends and roots and go off for a few years.

These were suggestions about where internationalists could be found. What I wanted, however, was a description of how to recognize one. I found it when I began to ask about qualities or characteristics that one might look for.

My interview subjects were describing people with a spirit of adventure—people who expressed joy in overcoming difficulties, who were flexible, curious, and open-minded. It didn't seem to be important that they were seeking an international position or even that they had expressed an interest on being hired. Neither was it significant, or even necessarily desirable, to find "country experts"—in reality, yet another technical specialty. What was important was the mindset. Descriptive words that interviewees used to characterize the internationalist mindset included *entrepreneurial, risk-taking, adventurous, adaptable, curious, flexible, values-based identification,* and *willing.* The regular occurrence of these words was one of the most significant and universal findings of the entire interview process.

Some of my most interesting interviewees put it in more streetwise terms. "If I meet a person who is more comfortable finding out about the local McDonald's in a city, I don't think they're going to be that successful because they are not willing to take that cultural leap and be interested in finding out what this place has to offer," said Linda Sweeney, a contract CFO, who has a list of international ventures to her credit.[7]

"Being an internationalist is not simply a state of mind, but also a state of body. And that body is in motion an awful lot," said Chris Murray, the fast-moving president of ABT, a rapidly growing high-tech firm.[8] Still another said, "In the end, it's fun, for the right people. There are a lot of people out there who stay miserable, but these are the people that would have difficulty moving from New Jersey to Iowa."

Strategic planning for internationalists should include looking beyond the borders of the country, a strategy mentioned by several Asian internationalists and a few North American executive level interviewees. An expatriate can come from anywhere to be sent anywhere else. "I think it fundamentally starts at a whole different level of thought about what your corporation is. If you are a global fisherman, you should recruit just as heavily at the entry level overseas as you do domestically," said Doug Williams, executive vice president of Chase Bank at their New York headquarters.[9]

There are some excellent reasons for recruiting talent from universities and technical institutes in other geographic regions. First, from an expansion standpoint, it's invaluable to have local managers who know both the corporate and cultural ropes. Foreign recruits can be brought into corporate headquarters to get "business of the business" training and to become steeped in the culture of their parent organization. They can subsequently prove invaluable in blending the corporate culture with their native culture. Sending them back into their own countries after this training period can also save a great deal of money and mitigate the risk of sending an expatriate from headquarters. The Harvard-AMROP survey found that "companies plan to rely heavily on recruiting host country nationals to fill these positions (in foreign subsidiaries). In addition, more than three-quarters expect to recruit candidates much earlier in their careers and then to develop them internally for posting to their home country."[10]

A practical tactic I heard about was to accept international degree students, either domestically or internationally, as volunteer interns in international operations. This can offer international experience and exposure to a new crop of potential internationalists preparing to be incorporated into companies' international tracks. The creation of internships can be structured to bring in students with specific language skills, knowledge bases, and other talents that are part of a corporate human resources initiative.

Another creative method of internationalizing is to seek talent from an immigrant population or from second-generation children of immigrants. Many of these people are bilingual and have a piece of both their cultures, the old and the new. They can provide an effective bridge for companies moving into new locations. An example is the Viet Kieu, Vietnamese people who either left Vietnam during the tragic war years or were born of émigré Vietnamese parents. Educated in other countries, some of these young professionals are now going back to Vietnam, which welcomes them, and they are creating an effective bridge for Western businesses moving into that changing nation. (This can be a tricky strategy, however, since some émigré groups are fiercely opposed to current regimes in their native countries, so they obviously would not be good places to recruit with the thought of sending people back to their roots.)

Mixing and blending nationalities and cultures inside a company is a creative method of "internationalizing by osmosis." It is one way of shifting the mindset and altering cultural programming, expanding minds and creating or encouraging a new crop of internationalists.

Growing your own: Internal recruiting

There wasn't a single best method mentioned by any of the interviewees when it came to recruiting internationalists. The fact was that many companies didn't deliberately recruit these people at all; instead, they tried to scare them up from inside the company when they were needed, usually basing the selection decisions on the technical skills that were important to the project at hand. Moreover, the decisions were likely to be made by someone other than human resources professionals.

A survey on global sourcing and selection practices, conducted by the National Foreign Trade Council (NFTC) and Selection Research International (SRI) in 1995, generated the following results: 94 percent of the respondents said line managers interviewed candidates; 96 percent rated technical requirements of the job and 94 percent rated business needs as the principal criteria used by their companies to select international candidates. The people responsible for selection decisions lacked appropriate assessment training, while the results of formal assessment procedures were little used.[11] This survey reported the results of questionnaire responses by 52 major western companies.

Another survey by NFTC and Windham International in 1996, with 192 respondents, supported these findings, indicating that 95 percent were evaluated by managers and 48 percent by HR interviews, with minimal attention being paid to formal internal or external assessments.[12]

Dr. Ruth Bleuzé of Prudential Intercultural Services, a company that provides high-quality cross-cultural training for businesses, commented:

*Ten years ago, 95 percent of those sent out were white
males forty-five years old, two kids, and a nonworking
spouse. Now, it's changing, but not dramatically—that
profile would cover 80 percent. More and more, now they
are younger, in their twenties and thirties, single people and
more women. Some say about 13 percent female, but we're
seeing only 6 to 7 percent in this organization. And for the
most part, white, young, and not married.*[13]

She added that the percentages of men and women were
somewhat industry-dependent, with more variety seen in the newer
industries. She indicated that the internationalist experience was
being pushed down to mid-management levels, whereas it had been
largely limited to executives in the past. But still, she said, people
with good technical skills are the ones being chosen, and they are
being chosen for those skills alone; she mentioned sales and
marketing, financial consultants, and auditors as examples.

The choices are typically made by the receiving managers or
by a team of sending and receiving managers. The human resources
department is generally not consulted, even though they are the
ones who are most aware of the significance of characteristics and
attitudes. They too are usually the ones who get panicky calls in the
middle of the night when international people and their families are
in crisis, unable to cope with cultural and business demands in a
foreign environment where the rules are unclear to them.

These problems arise in part because there is rarely any real
policy for hiring career-directed internationalists to start with. My
conversation with Bleuzé continued with a discussion of the career
intentions of those being sent out. I asked if her experience
indicated that they had planned for international careers. She
replied:

*By and large, no. There we go back to the way that the
corporation defines itself and recruits people, brings them
into, and orients them to the goals of the company. Some of
the younger ones are interested. But unfortunately, most of
them look forward to their assignment because they want to*

get their ticket punched. They know they're in a multinational corporation and in order to advance they need an international assignment. So they say "Send us somewhere, let us put in our two years, and we'll come back."[14]

Technical professionals and MBAs are educated in concrete methodology, whether in economics, scientific methods, engineering disciplines, or computer technology. They learn to think in structures and formulas, not in the vagaries of dealing with human beings with very diverse orientations. This is not to say that they won't do well. They can be quite successful if they possess internationalist characteristics and if they're prepared and coached well. Companies are taking an awful chance when they dispatch someone on an international assignment simply because he or she knows how to run a manufacturing plant or set up a factory. While people might develop into internationalists by default, learning and thriving in unusual situations, unless they have the characteristic curiosity and tolerance for ambiguity, even the best pre-departure training will merely give them additional knowledge. It will not help them to adapt and thrive. They can still fall prey to preset notions about how things *ought* to be and fail to cope with the differences they encounter. There are places in the world that are so exotic and so difficult, that to send people there merely in the hope they'll make it is a very expensive risk. The cost of providing assessment, first-class training, and ongoing support is a small fraction of total project costs. Look on it as insurance.

If the statistics on selection based primarily on technical criteria aren't dramatic enough, consider the second part of the equation. The Harvard-AMROP study's findings were stark. In international assignments that failed, 80 percent involved individuals who were unable to adjust to the culture; 70 percent found the demands of the job overwhelming; and in 69 percent, the expatriate family were unable to adjust.[15] And from NFTC/SRI: "96% of the respondents identified 'personality traits/interpersonal style' as the most important factors contributing to international assignment *failure*" (emphasis added).[16]

Simply stated, research shows that the vast majority of selections are made based on technical capabilities, and that the vast majority of failures are based on personality and interpersonal styles. Something is wrong with the selection criteria. We are back again to the corporate attitude about who is of value.

Clearly, the corporate mindset and practices have everything to do with finding the right people to use in international assignments. The myriad practical suggestions of my interviewees for finding them are excellent, as long as recruitment is followed by a system for assessing, preparing, and mobilizing them for both going out and coming back.

Internationalists on contract

There are adventurers for whom the whole world is a field for constant exploration and discovery, like a vast archeological dig. They want nothing more than to move continually from assignment to assignment. Endlessly curious, they are frequently on the fringe of their corporations and prefer to stay there. Their efforts to stay away from mundane desk jobs can frustrate managers seeking efficient use of corporate resources.

These people who value novelty over stability can, however, bring great energy, creativity, and adaptability to overseas projects. Some companies have begun to hire them as short-term or long-term specialized contract professionals who can take off for other parts of the world and stay for a few months or a few years. From the standpoint of organizational resources, this makes sense on both sides. Corporations can contract with specialists for term positions, and those specialists can manage their careers in a way that satisfies their need for worldwide exposure and new experiences. In recent years several companies have sprung up that specialize in placing term professionals, primarily technical and functional experts. Some of these placement companies specialize in a certain industry, such as computer science or telecommunications.

Regardless of where they are found, it's important to match the right one to the right job. It takes some strategic thinking to assess how to best use international talent, taking into consideration their own preferences as well as the needs of the company. The nature of an assignment can and should dictate what skills might be needed. Youth, energy, and an entrepreneurial spirit are appealing for a start-up venture, especially in a challenging region. A more mature and experienced internationalist would be a wise choice for an established venture that calls for a high level of management skill.

Tools for assessment and preparation

There are no completely foolproof methods for assessing whether a given individual will be successful internationally. There are, however, some profiling instruments that can help—especially when used in combination—to identify and coach people who are likely to succeed in an international assignment. Companies can rarely afford to invest the time and energy necessary to find the perfect match for a challenging assignment, but they should give serious attention to the personal characteristics of their potential assignees.

Here are two instruments I have used which I believe to be both reliable and useful. They can be administered to both the prospective internationalist and to family members who plan to go into the field.

Meyers-Briggs Type Indicator (MBTI)
This instrument is concerned with differences among people that result from the ways they focus attention, gather information, and make decisions, and the lifestyle they choose. The instrument has its earliest roots in the theories of Carl Jung and was originally published in the early 1960s. Since then it has been regularly revised and updated and has been used extensively in a wide variety of situations. A reliable tool, it is validated internationally and has been translated into many languages. It is easy to administer and score, readily available, and inexpensive, qualities which make it a good choice for budget-conscious companies. However, it does require a certified administrator and interpreter.

The MBTI should not be used for the purpose of selecting someone for an international assignment; rather, it is best employed to reveal behavioral preferences. However, the results of the MBTI can correlate with success in particular types of jobs because people with certain behavioral preferences tend to be attracted to particular functional areas of work. It is also a good tool for multi-cultural team development, since it reveals the behavioral preferences of each group member, turning up areas where differences in interpersonal communications and behaviors are likely to cause frustration and stress.

Once the analysis has been completed, a specialist can advise the potential internationalist how to use the results as a self-development guide or as the basis for working with a coach in preparation for an assignment.

There is not space here to delve deeply into the richness of this instrument. However, those seeking more information about it can turn to a number of good books on the MBTI. Among them are *Gifts Differing: Understanding Personality,* by Isabel Briggs Meyers; and *Please Understand Me: Character and Temperament Types,* by David Kiersey and Marilyn Bates.

Overseas Assignment Inventory (OAI)

Whereas the MBTI is a broad-based instrument with a multitude of uses, the Overseas Assignment Inventory (OAI) is specifically designed to be used in selecting, placing, and coaching international assignees. It measures attitudes and attributes that are directly related to cross-cultural adjustment. According to the research, which began with the development of the profile in the early 1970s and continues today, there is a strong correlation between high OAI scores and successful adjustment in international situations. The profile is based on data from several thousand naval personnel, Canadian technical advisers around the world, exchange students from the United States, Latin America, and Europe, more than 1,000 Peace Corps volunteers, and more than 4,500 corporate employees and their spouses. The instrument is meant to be administered to both the internationalist and his or her accompanying spouse, with the results interpreted by a well-trained coach.

This is a rich, multipurpose tool that can be used in a variety of ways. It can reveal the best choice from a pool of candidates; it can match attitudes and attributes of candidates to the requirements of specific international assignments; and it can match a candidate's strengths to cultural elements of the country for which he or she is being considered. It serves as an excellent coaching tool in providing guidance for potential internationalists or selectees in identifying possible problem areas and examining ways they can be mitigated. Finally, it can be used either before an international assignment or as a diagnostic tool in cases of on-the-job assignment difficulties.

Interestingly, the OAI also lends itself well to career development and career planning for companies that want to develop a pool of potential and appropriate internationalists—one of the areas where many international companies desperately need organizational development.

The OAI is a product of Prudential Intercultural and can be obtained from their offices in Westminster, Colorado. Corporate staff can be trained and certified to administer the instrument, but this is an expensive process, and its success is based extensively on the skill of the interpreter and coach. As an alternative, corporations can obtain qualified OAI interpreters directly from Prudential. In either case, the cost of the package is a fraction of the cost of a failed international assignment, which was calculated by the Harvard-Amrop study to be in excess of $300,000 for relocation alone.

Family concerns

The selection of internationalists can be complicated by family issues that may prevent an otherwise appropriate person from accepting an assignment or from successfully completing one. When an international assignment affects a family, the whole group should participate in the decision-making and interview processes. If the employee's spouse and children are kept informed—especially if they actively seek and anticipate an international assignment, and are adequately prepared for it—success is far more likely.

The survey conducted by NFTC/SRI reported dramatic findings concerning family members: "While the 'spouse's career' and 'family problems' were low on the list of selection criteria, these two factors were identified among the most critical contributing to failed/unsuccessful assignments."[17] The Harvard-Amrop study bore this out, finding that 69 percent of failures resulted at least in part from the inability of family members to adjust.[18] This strongly supports the need to assess *both* potential assignee and spouse.

Sending Them Out

The second challenge in recruiting internationalist talent is keeping them. Impatient to get going, young professionals bent on an international career may jump ship early if not given an assignment abroad. They don't want to stick around long enough to learn "the business of the business" —to gain organizational, systems, and product knowledge, as well as the seasoning they'll need to function well in the wider world. For this reason, it's important for companies to have a plan or career path and high-quality developmental programs in place to give this talented group the necessary exposure to the various aspects of the business.

High-potential internationalists need experience in many different types of situations, both cultural and organizational. With exposure to start-ups, joint ventures, and turn-arounds, in multicultural groups and teams, they can be given direct experience of a number of organizational challenges and can be rotated on short assignments through different places. Couple that with professional development programs to keep knowledge current and to cultivate leadership abilities.

Rotational assignments

Once internationalists are recognized as a unique corporate resource, and once an effort is made to identify and recruit them early as a method of globalizing the corporate resources, then companies will need a comprehensive developmental process to educate these recruits in the business operations and culture of the corporation, as well as to provide some kinds of field training. Some Asian executives with experience in large multinational corporations gave me advice regarding this process. They suggested that internationalist recruits work a short stint at corporate or regional headquarters, then go out to the field immediately, rotating on brief learning assignments through international locations. In that way they would gain exposure to the realities of international life while simultaneously getting practical experience in different aspects of the business. (This topic is addressed in more detail in chapter 5.)

Inpatriates are part of the rotational mix. As people move around internationally within an organization, in-place staff must work with them. Cross-cultural issues that come up for rotating internationalists also come up for those who work with them during their rotations. It is just as important to prepare home-based staff to work with these inpatriates, or incoming internationalists, as it is to prepare those doing the moving around. The following discussion of cross-cultural training should be applied to everyone in an organization who works with international staff.

Cross-cultural training programs

There a number of excellent intercultural training companies in many parts of the world that provide predeparture training, repatriation assistance, family preparation, team intervention and development. Many of them bring in host-country nationals to talk, answer questions, and coach the departing assignee and family, including children, about life and business practices in their countries. In addition, these consultants can provide ongoing team-building training for people on both sides of the business project. (More information on cross-cultural training and language studies can be found in chapter 5.)

It's a good investment to find a cross-cultural consultant with an established record of success, and make the investment. This kind of specialization isn't usually found in human resources departments. It's also important that cross-cultural assistance be available to internationalists in the field on a continuing basis, rather than being limited to a week-long predeparture class. These specialists are definitely helpful up front, but they are far more helpful if they can be called on at need during the course of an overseas assignment.

Experienced mentors

Returned or current internationalists are another excellent resource for those who are on the way to a foreign location. They can provide realistic information and preparation for the internationalists and their families. Ideally, this kind of partnership is formed between people exchanging places, or between an employee preparing for departure and one who has been out and back within the past year. The coaching can be carried on face to face, or via e-mail or telephone. The important thing is to link those going out with those who have been there. This mentor could continue to function as the at-home connection for the internationalist once he or she is actually on the job.

Relocation assistance

One of the most effective systems for moving people and families around the world has been designed—not surprisingly—by the U.S. military services. When an individual in the military is reassigned to a new location, the receiving unit designates a sponsor responsible for communicating with the incoming family. Depending on individual initiative, the sponsor may go to great lengths. They can help find lodging, welcome the newcomers at the airport, make introductions, connect them in social circles, and act as cultural informants on such matters as transportation, language study, shopping, and everyday services. They may assist with any of the matters of daily life that have to be relearned in a new country. It's an enormous help and a huge relief to families trying to cope with the stresses of moving, new jobs, and new countries.

This system is perfectly suited for adoption by corporations. It can be a very useful tool when internationalists are being sent to countries where there is already an established workforce. It can work equally well when they return or move on. (See the following discussion of repatriation.)

Keeping the Internationalist in the Corporate Mainstream

Fortunately, corporations have moved away from the disastrous strategy of sending people abroad just to get rid of them. They have learned not to send anyone out whom they don't want back. This means that the expatriate must be maintained in mind and spirit as a vital member of the corporate community who will rejoin it physically after the assignment.

International assignments take people away from the mainstream of their corporations, which removes them from the center of influence and limits their ability to make advantageous political and career moves. Unless a corporation establishes a career path and an organizational system to support international assignments, it will continue to have difficulty in finding fully qualified candidates who will accept an international project.

For many years my business has been people and their work. While working in the outplacement business, I had occasion to visit with executives and managers who had left companies after international assignments. Most of these former expatriates talked about the difficulties of returning to the corporate home only to find that they had been left on the sidelines, completely out of touch. They had lost their power base and their networks. Their international assignments were not valued, and there was no longer a place for them in the company. No one knew or appreciated the value of what they did while they were "out there," and no one wanted to hear about it. Out of sight was also out of mind. Not only does the organization lose the internationalist in these cases, along with the accumulated knowledge and experience, but others inside witness this fall-out. It is a dramatic disincentive for talented people who may be considering a cross-border assignment.

How can a company prevent this dissatisfaction, which is likely to result in the loss of a valuable employee? Here is a strategy that has worked.

A home-based mentor can be recruited and assigned, formally or informally, to the departing employee, with the agreement that the mentor will provide a flow of information to the colleague abroad.

The Internationalists

This information flow can operate through regular telephone calls, forwarding corporate e-mail, sending newsletters, or even passing on "water-cooler" conversations. This base-touching keeps the internationalist aware of events and trends at headquarters. The mentor can offer advice, assess the political climate and other changing elements, and keep the internationalist in tune with developments in the corporate culture. If the mentor departs before the internationalist returns, the corporation should provide a new mentor to make sure that the information flow continues.

These relationships can work extremely well as long as the home-based mentor keeps his side of the bargain and takes the responsibility seriously. If both parties structure an agreement before the internationalist departs, it is more likely to be of real ongoing benefit. It helps if mentoring responsibilities can be made part of the home-based individual's performance objectives—criteria on which he or she will be evaluated. This technique is very effective because it builds a definite role with stated responsibilities and accountability.

Bringing Them Back

In a study by the Conference Board on returning expatriates from 152 companies, more than 80 percent of returnees said that they believed their corporate parent placed little or no value on their international experience. Author and consultant Craig Sorti found that 25 percent of returning expatriates left their companies within a year of coming home, resulting in a huge drain of internationalist talent. In addition, a whopping 46 percent said they had less autonomy or authority at home than in the international assignment; 75 percent experienced a reduced standard of living on return; and only 12 percent received promotions.[19] These data represent U.S. companies, but according to some interviewees, much the same pattern is prevalent in other Western nations.

Tom Fahey told me:

> *The biggest problem is the reverse culture shock of the returning executive. He gets back to the home office and*

goes bonkers. The main syndrome of the returned executive with problems is climbing the walls. He's used to calling the shots, and now he's got to clear it with twelve people in the home office.

Many interviewees expressed frustration at failing to find talented, skilled people who would accept international assignments. This failure was directly related to the value placed on these assignments and how returning internationalists were reintegrated into the company. People respond to the realities they see and experience, not to lip service. It is a sad fact that many returned expatriates feel that they have made a professional and personal sacrifice for an unappreciative company. Clearly, the more value a company puts on the international career, the more value they will receive in return from employees who will not only accept but also succeed in assignments abroad.

Some experienced multinationals have developed simple and effective repatriation plans that help returnees reincorporate. It does, however, take effort on both sides for such a plan to work effectively. Ideally, a full-circle internal process should be designed to provide a route for internationalists to navigate the corporate waters and manage a successful international assignment, then return. This "out-and-in" circle is presented conceptually in the figure below.

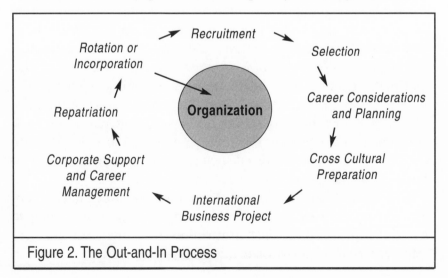

Figure 2. The Out-and-In Process

If a mentor has been working with the internationalist since departure and is still in place at the time of return, then the responsibility for helping with re-entry belongs with that individual. If the mentorship role has been absent or weak, a sponsor can be sought to help with the return.

The sponsor coordinates with human resources to make sure the returnee is positioned several months in advance for consideration for any appropriate openings. These might be short-term projects in the home location to begin the reintegration process. Again, the communication flow should continue, with the sponsor informing the returnee about the politics, changes, and flavor of the corporate home. When the internationalist returns, the sponsor continues to serve as a guide back into the system. Sponsors can provide internal exposure for returnees by helping to identify forums in which they can share their knowledge and gain internal exposure to help with their reintegration. In this win-win solution, both returnee and company gain.

Kevin Taylor, international sales manager in Latin America for Snorkel, a manufacturer of aerial work platforms, summed up the contributions of the returning expatriate: "The value I bring is, I bring the outside in. I bring the international market to headquarters."[20]

A common lament of returned internationalists—as well as those who are currently out in the world—is that their corporation doesn't really know what to do with their accumulated knowledge and skills. There are several good reasons to tackle this problem internally. First, these employees have a storehouse of knowledge and understanding that should be institutionalized if companies want to foster a global outlook internally. Second, showcasing them internally shows that high regard and value are placed on their positions and experience; this attitude will go a long way toward dispelling the reluctance of talented managers to consider international assignments.

It's smart to give public value to those who work internationally. Psychologically, kudos for the former field person can help to avert the dislocation and disaffection that often affect these returnees. And organizationally, it acknowledges their value in full view of the rest of the workforce and encourages others to seek this recognition.

Following are some of the ideas and practices suggested by the interviewees.

Debriefing and advising

As internationalists return, their company can bring them together with "debriefing boards" of strategic planners to gather their firsthand insights on how things are going, why money is being made or lost, how the foreign partners are working out, and how the company can manipulate the situation more favorably. A concurrent human resources debriefing board can gather returnees' perceptions of the personalities involved, what kinds of human or cultural situations are arising, and what training strategies might be effective.

An internal commission or organization of experienced inter-nationalists can act as an advisory board for corporate strategic planners, for people in the field, and for departing and returning expatriates. This group can decide how their talents can best be used to advance the image and capabilities of the company. Showcase them at internal meetings and conferences to talk about their experiences, their problems, and how they solved (or didn't solve) them. Hindsight is twenty-twenty: let them talk about what alternatives could have been employed, or how they think it *should* have been done. And most of all, listen to what they say.

Creative leadership

International assignments hone creative problem-solving skills. Let the people engaged in international assignments come together to share ideas and solutions and best practices with each other. Bring the group of project leaders together regularly, both during projects and after, to talk about successes and issues and brainstorm with each other. Bring them inside for organizational meetings so they stay in tune with what's going on at headquarters and around the world. Their unique perspective can bring fresh thinking to internal problems. It is yet another way to show recognition and value for their skills and to institutionalize their knowledge.

The returnee's responsibility

Once internationalists have actually returned, they have the responsibility to readjust if they want to stay with the company. This might mean that a returning executive must accept a position with less autonomy than he or she formerly exercised. The returned internationalist may need to devote renewed energy to the adaptive skills of flexibility and openness to new experiences.

Another side to this out-and-back story appeared in several interviews: returning internationalists came back with an "attitude." Accustomed to being in charge of their own kingdom, they returned expecting promotions and increased responsibilities. However, they frequently were unaware of what was going on in the home office and were very disappointed and disillusioned when nothing was available that they thought worthy of their talents. Senior-level positions are not numerous in any company and are difficult and challenging to get. (One might argue, however, that senior positions in an international company *should* be filled by people with international experience.)

Unhappy circumstances like this have their roots in the preparation stage for international assignments. Before internationalists depart, their path to return should be reviewed realistically by their managers and human resources so that expectations are not out of line with reality.

Tom Fahey pointed out:

> *Business goes through cycles. And except in recent years, half of the time you're in a down-cycle and half of the time you're in an up-cycle. So when it's time for you to come back, or when circumstances bring you back, 50 percent odds are that you're in a down-cycle. They're laying people off, they're downsizing, and they don't know what to do with you. Look at it this way, it's a big risk when you go overseas*

for other reasons, too. So when it's time for you to come back and the company is in a down-cycle, they may put you in a back windowless office and give you three months to find yourself a job in the company, or adios. That happens all the time.

This means, then, that there is a responsibility on the part of the internationalist who returns. It requires a continuous effort to stay connected and in touch with what's happening at headquarters while the employee is abroad.

During an overseas assignment, people learn skills and employ talents that earn them their stripes as internationalists. However, they also need to learn how to talk about what they know, and how and where it can be applied within an organizational context. On return, it will be their responsibility to apply their newly honed skills—both personal and technical—to best advantage. Keeping lines of communication open is vital.

Linda Sweeney advises:

People at the home office have several joint ventures on the boards and they're trying to monitor a whole bunch of different projects. So you have to be very direct in getting your point across about what you need, what's going well, what isn't. I would spend time making sure the people back home knew what was going on. Sometimes when you work a sixteen-hour day just trying to get the local stuff done, you forget about building these relationships, networking with the people who are actually holding the purse strings. And it's important. You really have to do it. Make the time.

In Western organizations, where competitiveness and individuality are hallmarks of behavior, people need to blow their own horns and to stay in touch in the right places. It's a common complaint of returning internationalists that "out of sight is out of mind." How they can stay visible while they're physically elsewhere?

A number of career management strategies can be employed. Make use of the mentor in the corporate home, who should be in touch and in tune, informing the internationalist of internal events and the political climate. Home leave is an ideal time to renew acquaintances and contacts. Visits around the offices, contacts with the HR department, and social engagements are all useful in maintaining visibility. Regular communication is critical, especially when repatriation time nears. Several months before returning, it's wise to begin working with the HR department to find out what opportunities are coming up and to express preferences for reassignment. It's challenging, to be sure, but it dramatically reduces the repatriation syndrome.

Permanent Expatriates

Sometimes internationalists don't want to come back at all. Just as some can't adapt to another culture, others find that their new setting fulfills deep-seated dreams. Internationalists must try to dig in deeply enough to begin to think like the people in the foreign culture in order to communicate effectively and work with the differences. At the same time, they must maintain enough distance to see their local project in the larger perspective of global business purposes. It's not an easy task. Some have "gone native" and found it preferable not to return. They sometimes marry abroad, have a family, and spend a lot of time finding ways to avoid returning to the corporate home. In such cases, a corporation might choose to leave a valuable person in the field rather than risk losing one by insisting on return. The corporation may be able to move the internationalist into the status of a local national and adjust salary and benefits accordingly, thus keeping a valuable contributor and saving the expense of maintaining an expatriate.

Summary

Worldwide and world-class companies should value their internationalists. Leaders must drive the vision and mindset of the company, changing insular approaches and implementing policies that encourage and reward international involvement on the part of skilled managers.

Good internationalists possess the characteristics of curiosity, risk-taking, and entrepreneurial spirit; they thrive on change and ambiguity. Corporate leaders must actively promote—not just give lip service to—a culture that encourages and rewards creativity and innovation, risk-taking and new ideas, lest companies find themselves with an employee base rooted in bureaucracy and unable or unwilling to take any risks or make any changes.

Success in international ventures requires cooperation between the selecting organization and the selected internationalist. Each has a responsibility to the other to implement or carry on the foreign business venture, to communicate, and to move on. Planning and common sense on both sides can prevent pain and unwelcome surprises.

Leaders have an imperative need to promote and reward behaviors that encourage potential internationalists to come on board and stick with them. They must:

- recognize who the internationalists are;
- define roles for them in the company;
- acquire a methodology for developing them;
- establish a plan for sending them out and bringing them back successfully; and
- use their accumulated wisdom and recognize them within their constituencies.

Leaders have the responsibility for overall company performance, including the international elements. It's time for the internationalist in global strategy to be not merely recognized but accorded a vital role in achieving corporate goals. These are the new professionals for a new century.

3

The Close-Up:
Internationalists in the Field

We don't see things as they are. We see things as we are.

—Anaïs Nin

Passports evoke the exotic and release the adrenalin of adventure. Travelers are beckoned to imbibe art, language, music, food, and architecture. Cameras capture the beauty of foreign places, and the visible contrasts between cultures are revealed in fascinating detail. The traveler returns with mementos and memories to cherish for years.

Then the same traveler is off on a business trip, a venture involving two or more organizations from different countries. Suddenly the excitement and appeal of an international holiday are overwhelmed by the complexities of negotiations, contracts, agreements, and business practices. Casual becomes formal, and tolerance gives way to demands. What was fascinating in leisure becomes frustrating in business.

During my travels and interviews, people took one nearly universal position regarding foreigners coming into their countries for business purposes. It was, quite simply, "They must understand us." When I asked them to elaborate, their responses indicated that they were referring to culture, traditions, and values as well as to legal standards and business practices. They talked about both national and organizational cultures. They also stressed the importance of language and the need for business people to have, at a minimum, a working knowledge of the local tongue.

In this chapter culture differences are uncovered as a manageable way of approaching the infinite variety of human encounters faced by international work groups. Anecdotes clarify the ways these differences are manifested and viewed in ordinary business situations. These examples—only a few of the hundreds related to me by internationalists—testify to the myriad circumstances that require the combination of internationalist characteristics and technical competency. It's what happens "out there."

Everyone's reality is culture-bound. To a foreigner in unfamiliar situations and surroundings, things may not seem real or right. The internationalist characteristics of tolerance, flexibility, curiosity, and the ability to deal with ambiguity, are absolutely essential in coming to terms with this kind of dislocation, or "culture shock." It is how people act, react, come together, or stay at odds that makes for success or failure.

> Culture is a system of understandings that is shared and transmitted within a group.

The concept of culture embraces everything human beings do that is not dictated by their biological characteristics. Language, art, religion, agriculture, industry, trade, social relations, education— all these and many more aspects of human life are elements of culture, and all of them vary from place to place and from time to time. No culture is really static, and today cultures are changing more rapidly than ever.

The people who share a culture share not just knowledge and skills, but also behaviors and values. The latter are harder to explain to outsiders—in part because many people never realize that their patterns of communication or their ethical beliefs could be different from those of other cultures. It is the role of social scientists, including anthropologists, linguists, and sociologists, to analyze and identify the differences among cultures and help people understand one another. It is the role of businesspeople to anticipate them, learn about them, and creatively manage them.

It is crucial to realize that most individuals belong to several cultural groups simultaneously. In some parts of the world, people tend to identify with a national or regional culture; in others, ethnic origin may be more important than nation-state citizenship. Cultural practices and outlooks may differ according to socioeconomic status, age, education, religion, or profession. Stop and consider the difference you would expect to find in the United States between a group of elderly bankers and a group of young wildlife biologists: they might be more different than two groups of bankers, or biologists, from the United States and Iran.

An internationalist going into the field can't hope to master the intricacies of another culture completely and quickly. However, the process will be facilitated by identifying the areas where cultures often differ—especially those areas that impinge directly on business success.

Two Kinds of Culture: Organizational and National

When people say that the inhabitants of a certain nation or region behave differently in some way, they are actually talking about universal behaviors exhibited to different degrees. If we can identify and name a behavioral characteristic, it is probably displayed to some extent by all humans. Thus, we may claim that the British and Germans are more assertive, outspoken, and comfortable speaking up to their bosses than are Thai or Chinese people; however, a wide range of assertiveness exists in all four populations, and you could well find an outspoken Chinese partner in your working group, or a diffident German.

People find it irresistible to form *stereotypes* or descriptions of "typical" members of nationalities and ethnic groups. Even though experts in human relations discourage this tendency, it has gone on throughout human history and will probably have a hold on us for a while longer. Stereotypes may be applied from within a culture as well as from without: how often have you heard statements like "We Italians are a passionate people"? Nearly everyone has heard about the emotional Latins, the arrogant French, the aggressive Americans, and the inscrutable Asians.

Within each society or culture, some people will behave like their stereotype and some will not. It is not possible to anticipate accurately how individuals will behave, no matter where they come from. The respected intercultural researcher Geert Hofstede has stated, "Computers may be programmed the same way, but minds most certainly are not."[1]

People also belong to smaller cultural groups within their larger ones. Among them are government and business organizations. The internationalists I talked with often emphasized that their challenges resulted as much from clashes between organizational cultures as from those between national cultures. They report an "us versus them" attitude, with team members from one organization finding fault with those from the other. It's tough to start from these divided beginnings and create a unique new culture that is a blend of more than one organizational culture and more than one national culture. To further complicate matters, each business encounter, each team effort will be different. In any new business venture, even within the same organization, the situations encountered won't be duplicates of previous ones.

The elusive goal is to move a group from the divided "us versus them" mentality to the cohesiveness of a new, single, functioning unit with its *own* distinct culture. Dutch author Fons Trompenaars has written, "International managers have it tough. They must operate on a number of different premises at any one time. These premises arise from their culture of origin, the culture in which they are working, and the culture of the organization which employs them."[2] We can extend this to say that all members of a team, not just its leaders, operate with a mélange of cultural inputs.

The phrase "cultural differences" usually brings to mind things that can be clearly seen or heard, like music, language, literature, architecture, dress, or food. Not so easily observed are deeply engrained ways of expressing (or not expressing) individuality, handling conflict or negotiating, dealing with authority, expressing emotions, communicating to indicate respect, valuing family and friends, or relating to time. On another level, differences in organizational culture have evolved from years of habit or deliberately orchestrated practices, anchored by rules both written and unwritten. It is these all-too-human issues that are the most problematic for companies building international alliances, because they involve differences in the perception of reality—of what is "normal" or "right."

Merely researching a culture before diving into a business venture won't provide a sufficiently complete picture. Work groups may be made up of individuals from different countries, and within those countries there are more layers of culture. Religious affiliation, age, education, gender, and ethnicity are only a few of the variables that can affect individuals inside a larger national culture. Add the layer of the distinct organizational structures from which team members come, and just imagine the muddle that cross-border projects can generate! Organizational differences regularly create communication problems if the team members do not understand the structure and behavior of the companies as well as the countries from which their collaborators come.

Differences Visible and Hidden

Differences come in several flavors. Some things can be easily seen by the casual tourist. Others can't be seen at all: you never know they exist until you run headlong into them the first time you meet with a new business team and try to get a decision made. Suddenly, you can't get the young Asian computer genius to speak out and express an opinion; at the same time, the Dutch scientist has most of the answers and doesn't hesitate to say so.

Consider this mass of cultural variables as an island. You can see the part that projects above the waves, but you can't see the part below. What you can't see, however, provides the *foundation* for what is visible. It's much the same with culture and behaviors. How

Figure 3. The National/Regional Island

Food	Art
Books	Music
Language	Greetings
Architecture	Celebrations
Style and Dress	Public Figures
Public Behavior	Public Social Functions
Magazines and Newspapers	

Taboos	Cultural Heroes
Political Issues	Male/Female Roles
Sense of Urgency	Importance of Family
Respect for Authority	Importance of History
Respect for Traditions	Tolerance for Ambiguity
Formality/Informality	Managing Conflicts/Differences
Significance of Religion	Importance of Age/Generations
Tolerance for Differences	Meaning of Gestures/Body Language
Importance of Relationships	Individuality vs. Group Consciousness

people behave, how they think, how they learn—virtually all their interactions with others—are based on the conditioning they grew up with. This is their reality. Look at the "island" figures: what you don't see is far more significant in business than what you do see.

Figure 4. The Organizational Island

Knots and Tangles

My consultants confirmed the findings of researchers that the three areas causing continuous problems for internationalists are:

- Relationships between people
- The concept of time
- Communication styles—how we say what we say

These aren't new concepts. They were identified in the early twentieth century, and they have been experienced by innumerable international businesspeople for far longer. Although my interviewees, academic researchers, and other authors approach these topics from different perspectives, the basics remain the same.

Definitions of cultural differences are meaningful only if they can be used and interpreted creatively to solve problems, and if people can see and anticipate some real-world ways in which these differences affect their lives and economic concerns. The following observations and anecdotes are typical of the encounters international businesspeople have experienced. (Much more detailed information is available about the intricacies of cross-cultural interactions; see the bibliography for some good sources.)

It is important to remember that generalizations about cultural differences apply better to entire *groups* of people than to particular individuals. There is always a continuum of variation, like a bell curve; however, the point at which the curve peaks is likely to vary from culture to culture.

Relationships between people

Most intercultural clashes involve this very large domain, relationships between people. In the following section, excerpts from interviews with internationalists and multicultural team members illustrate what occurs when cultural assumptions conflict. It is not an easy task to sort out and identify all the factors in an interaction, because many assumptions are linked and operate simultaneously. As you will see, no one country, nationality, or organization has a monopoly on behaviors that annoy others.

We have our own ways..

Adaptable and *definite* are two ends of an attitudinal continuum. On one end there are many possibilities, and on the other there are defined, prescribed standards. It can also be expressed as the level of tolerance for ambiguity and it can apply to individuals and organizations as well as to national cultures.

In *adaptable* cultures, people tend to deal well (or reasonably well) with ambiguous situations; they can seek and find better alternatives; in Western jargon, they can "roll with the punches." They manage well in uncertain situations and can improvise as unexpected situations emerge. At the extreme, adaptability can become an obsession with novelty, a constant re-creation and upending of the status quo—something Western businesses were occasionally accused of during interviews with non-Westerners.

Definite, the opposite end of the scale, characterizes cultures that require rules, both written and unwritten, and established, recognized ways of doing things. People from these cultures might resist change or insist on defined structures, roles, and tasks; people from more adaptable cultures might see them as culture- and tradition-bound. They become stressed when required to deal with the unknown, or when they are uncertain about the appropriate rules of behavior in a situation.

Areas of business that are affected by adaptability vs. definiteness include:

- resistance to or comfort with change
- mobility of employees
- level of risk-taking
- conformity to established rules
- micromanagement vs. delegation
- ability to deal directly with conflict within work groups

Researcher and author Geert Hofstede's extensive study of IBM employees in 53 countries, 72 subsidiaries, 38 occupations, and 20 languages identified different levels of a characteristic he calls "uncertainty avoidance," which corresponds to the adaptable—definite continuum.[3] Subjects with high uncertainty avoidance preferred to have policies and procedures firmly in place and not to be required to bend the rules to cope with unusual situations. The three anecdotal accounts below show how differing levels of adaptability and openness to innovation caused problems in international ventures.

The products were made in the U.S., shipped to Mexico, distributed and sold to Mexican industry. We discovered a lot of products we were bringing into Mexico were actually assembled in Mexico, in fact just down the street from our warehouse there. Why would we go through an eighteen-step logistics plan, incur additional 18 percent cost of getting products to the U.S.A., then back down to Mexico, when we could just have a truck drive down and deliver it to the warehouse in the first place? Well, the problem was convincing our product development team [at U.S. head-quarters]. That's the way it's always been done. Period. The problem was getting them to look beyond that."

Industrial product sales, United States/Mexico

The first month we had a problem where there was a fire. Since we were restructuring, the guy there didn't know what to do because of all the new people, so he called directly to the insurance department and they arranged everything. A month later, the boss of the boss of the boss of this guy sent me a letter telling me he was very upset because these guys solved the issue between themselves and he didn't know anything about it. He put the case to the Executive Committee and they wrote a rule, a procedures manual. Each situation had a number and said how you have to proceed up one side and down the other. That had to be followed in this company for three years.

Telecommunications, Argentina

For a successful factory, the place is very important. We were thinking which is better, Tijuana or Juarez? There is only one Japanese restaurant in Juarez and [they served] tempura with cucumbers! So Tijuana has a ramen shop, many noodle shops, and in San Diego, Japanese restaurants. That's why we selected Tijuana. Japanese people can't stay five years [where they don't have the right food].
Electronics manufacturer, Japan/Mexico

Interestingly, Hofstede's IBM study found that the cultures that were less flexible in conforming to written and unwritten rules of behavior were also more anxious (perhaps because they worried about breaking rules).

Father knows best

"Attitude toward authority" refers to degree of comfort that employees or team members feel in interactions with people they perceive to be dominant over them. Hofstede's IBM study calls this measure "power distance," or the degree to which individuals depend on authority figures. He found a high degree of deference to authority figures among Mediterranean, Latin American, Asian, and Arab employees, and low dependence on authority among Anglo (English and American), Germanic, and non-Mediterranean European subjects.

Deference relations are important in all cultures, but they are also quite varied. It is obvious that they can have profound effects on business operations, where some kind of hierarchical structure is almost always present.

Attitude toward authority affects such business activities as:

*   brainstorming
*   making decisions about procedures
*   giving and receiving feedback
*   negotiating
*   expressing opinions
*   managing conflict

The interview excerpts below show how two Americans and two Asians commented on their experiences with authority and deference.

> *If they had a better idea, they would express it to me, not to their own supervisors. I had to go to the managers and say this is what we are going to do. The workers couldn't go themselves. I was a big potato. It was okay for me to go to the boss, but not okay for them to go. They would never have considered questioning what they were told.*
> Construction products manufacturing, USA /China

> *The whole hierarchical thing. In meetings, the tables are all long and skinny. They arrive in order of importance, the most important guy comes in last and sits at the head. His lieutenants sit next to him. You don't sit just anywhere. It's the same in how you speak during meetings. You can't ask questions to clarify something. There can be some polite conversation, but no critical thinking, brainstorming or challenging.*
> Telecommunications joint venture, USA /Indonesia

> *People here don't like debate or argument. If you are not in a position of power and you're talking to a boss, you don't argue.*
> Petroleum industry, Malaysia

> *First we select the man who graduated from one of the top universities in Japan, very educated person. If the boss is a highly educated man, he will be very successful. The staff will obey him.*
> Electronics manufacturing, Japan

The two Americans quoted above had a negative view of what they perceived as unusual or even excessive deference. In many modern Western industries, employees at all levels are encouraged to contribute good ideas, ask questions, and critique plans, but these expatriates found a different system operating in Asia. By contrast, the Malaysian executive used a negative concept—"argument"—to characterize what the Americans might call "constructive interaction." The Japanese interviewee comments on prestigious education as one factor that stimulates deference in his society; although an American graduate of Harvard might have a similar advantage initially, her acceptance in a firm might be less unquestioning.

Who's important—what's important?

Western business culture is characterized by a high degree of individualism. Personal initiative, taking responsibility and action, and individual achievement are highly valued. There is competition between individuals as well as between organizations and divisions of organizations. This orientation is particularly strong in the United States and other formerly colonial societies where pioneering, fighting against the odds, and "rugged individualism" have historically been advantageous.

Many other cultures are more strongly influenced by group orientation, or affiliative culture, in which attitudes and behaviors are more centered on the concerns of society as a whole, or on groups within that society or organization. People in these cultures are likely to work in a single organization throughout their careers. In return for job security, they devote great loyalty to their employer.

The areas of business most commonly affected by the individualism/affiliation continuum are:

- management style and expectations
- decision-making processes
- personal responsibility and initiative

An expatriate coming into a more affiliative culture may be perceived as rude and uncaring, as this expatriate discovered:

I found out only after I asked repeatedly that I had offended nearly everyone in the office because I didn't say good morning to each person when I came in every day.

Minerals exploration, Canada/Brazil

Cultures that are more individualist in their orientation, typically North American, Northern European and Germanic, also tend to emphasize a precise methodology which relies heavily on scientific laws, as described in chapter 1. People with this approach apply logic to analyze, interpret, hypothesize, and predict. They see themselves as the point of control and take charge of their environments, lives, and businesses. They view success as a result of the proper application of internal energies. Once they have established strategies, they do not change or adapt them quickly. Many Western leaders apply this type of management inside their companies—often with great success, as long as they are operating in an environment where this kind of behavior is expected and readily accepted.

In a group-oriented culture, such as Latin American, Mediterranean and Asian, where personal relationships and group concerns are more prevalent, employees may seem to accept management dictates, but then nothing happens. Policies such as pay-for-performance, set sales goals, or project timelines may not work well because they don't take into account external circumstances that affect the individual's or the group's ability to achieve them. Dictates interrupt the flow of relationships. In a team situation, demands from outside the affiliative group can be seen as arrogant and aggressive, coming from people who don't truly understand what the group is dealing with. If the group members have a great deal of solidarity (a "we" instead of "I" orientation) and a strong need for harmony, they may meet such dictates with nods and seeming agreement, but little action.

In the excerpts below, an American and two Asians analyze the way this desire for surface harmony can create confusion in cross-cultural interactions:

> *They smile, they never argue, but they will drag their feet and not discuss anything. They agree and nod, but nothing changes. They won't tell you something that bothers them. They ignore anger. They consistently avoid, disappear, won't confront.*
>
> Telecommunications joint venture, USA/Indonesia

In a culture where people want to be nice to you, they won't say no. It's part of face-saving. It's conflict avoidance.

Human resources, Malaysia

Chinese like to say, "Okay, okay, okay." "Okay" doesn't mean he agreed. "Okay" means "I understand what you are saying now." We hate arguments. We hate disagreements in meetings.

Market research, Taiwan

Notice that the American uses negative words to characterize this behavior: "drag their feet," "avoid," "disappear." The Asians, however, regard the same behavior as "being nice" and "understanding what you are saying." Comparing different perceptions of the same behavior, as this small example does, is a good way to identify the point at which an interaction has gone wrong.

Relationship-building is profoundly affected by this dimension. In some Western cultures the attitude is direct and straightforward: "Let's get straight to the point and get to work." This attitude can cause considerable discomfort for international venture partners from more affiliative societies. They may actually refuse to do business without establishing the kind of relationship that is usual in their society. This can mean socializing, visiting with the family, and spending time getting to know one's counterparts on a personal level; during this period of adjustment, business may not be discussed at all.

Many of my interviewees spoke of the need to build a solid foundation of trust, and a few cited a very practical reason why certain societies required this. In countries where the judicial system historically has not been reliable, business could continue only between individuals who trusted each other implicitly. They could not rely on the courts for impartial protection of business interests. Even where progress has been made in subjecting business to the rule of law, the traditions of cementing relationships with gifts, favors, and shared social experiences can persist.

In this country, there is a way to greet people even when you go into a bar. You can't just start in with somebody ... with the business. There's a way of doing all that stuff. I think it's very difficult to deal with a client when the first thing you do is unexpected.

Law and consulting, Czech Republic

In Japan, when I inherited this distribution partnership, I was invited to the home of the president and introduced to the traditional tea ceremony where the wife or daughter would come on their knees into the room. It was completely traditional. This was a big honor and we really understood that we were fully adopted into the family and the business.

Consumer products manufacturing and distribution, USA /Japan

Being task-driven doesn't get you very far when you need to engage the hearts and minds of the people. You have to establish a relationship of comfort. You've got to be my friend. If you aren't my friend, how can I work with you? It's the way we do things.

Petroleum industry, Malaysia

Background ... you always hear that. Relationships are important. My advice is, go to a nice bistro with your partner, order a bottle of wine. Sit down and listen to what he has to say about his country. Enjoy it. Don't listen to it with other motives. Listen ... learn. And at the time that is right for them, they will come forward with this business. Patience. Patience and flexibility.

Construction equipment distribution, USA/Latin America

Always connect with the people first—try to understand what makes them tick, where they went to school, which clique they're in. Develop warm fuzzies before you talk business. Most Americans just get in there and do business—and I can just see those minds closing up. Click,

click … the doors just closing. I can sit there and watch this going on. It's so basic. It's really important.

Consumer products manufacturing, USA/China

I had experience in Latin America and you would not think of beginning to discuss an acquisition or joint venture, or any kind of sharing relationship until they meet you and understand what you're all about. That includes where you came from and your background. You have some common-alities from a social standpoint.

Office products, USA/Asia-Pacific/Europe

The people quoted above all realize that they need to construct personal and social relationships with their foreign colleagues before they begin business negotiations. They urge you both to listen and to respond by sharing something of yourself. It's one thing to say you have a lot in common with your foreign partners; it's quite another, more valuable thing to *show* that you do.

Group versus individual orientation also dictates the way a culture approaches decision-making. Affiliative groups tend to take a long time to reach a conclusion about a course of action because everyone must be consulted before a decision is reached — a practice that drives Western businesspeople crazy. This need for consensus is simply a result of concern for the needs of the group and the desire for agreement and harmony.

When we wanted to make a decision about taking a product to the market, they [Japanese] always said "We must discuss." Always. It took forever. I found that with the Japanese, they planned this long [indicating a three-foot armspan] and implemented this long [a one-foot span]. The Americans are just the opposite. I felt like we were always wasting at least one whole season getting products out.

Food and beverage distribution, Japan/USA.

This example illustrates an interesting dilemma. On one hand, moving quickly has market advantages. On the other hand, moving

The Internationalists

too fast can result in mistakes and a need to start over, which extends the implementation phase. Internationalist flexibility can help to negotiate a balance between the needs of the indigenous group and the needs of the business: the gasket that seals the two sides together.

The question of face

One of the most important factors in cross-border business relationships is the whole concept of "face." As social scientists use the term, face is the impression we convey of ourselves to others. Just as the physical face is the part of a person most exposed to view, communicative face is the aspect of a person most exposed to the judgment of others. Westerners tend to think of face as an Asian phenomenon, but it is actually at work in all human cultures, including Anglo. However, there is variability in the strategies associated with it and the importance attached to it.

In some cultures, a certain amount of mistake-making is acceptable. It's how we learn, so we are comfortable talking about it. But in others, such as Japan, to point out someone's mistake publicly is a terrible insult. Errors must be dealt with very differently to avoid causing anyone to lose face. Understanding the more powerful need to maintain face can be a very challenging issue to Westerners operating in Asia, as the following observations show:

> *If there was any kind of disagreement, you had to work it out so that it disappeared. There could be no confrontation.*
>
> Industrial products manufacturing, USA /China

> *People don't like conflicts. They would lose their face, and you'd look bad, too. And you're supposed to respect your supervisor—to give them face. If you do something that violates that, he'll make you pay.*
>
> Publishing, Taiwan

My experience interviewing executives in Japan was a practical demonstration of the strong need to maintain face. I wanted to hear about business issues and challenges they encountered while involved in international business situations. To judge from their stories, however, all was not only good but completely without difficulties. They were exceedingly gracious and welcoming, and I was so charmed that I didn't realize they had told me interesting stories that really revealed nothing until I began to transcribe and analyze the interviews.

One size fits all

It's easy to know what's right and what's wrong. Right? Wrong. This refers to what Trompenaars calls the "universalist-particularist" dimension of culture. Simply stated, this is the notion that rules are rules and should apply to everyone, all the time. Moreover, if a system works in one place, it will work equally well everywhere else. This has been the overriding viewpoint in Western society (Anglo, Northern European, Germanic) for many centuries. Fortunately, however, the position is now being challenged by businesses who have discovered the inherent difficulties in attempting to apply the same rules all over the world.

Travelers may be startled, and even amused, when a minor event illustrates this cultural difference. Germans are often stereotyped as extremely rule-bound, and Americans as minor rule-breakers, especially when it is convenient or saves time.

> *I remember waiting to cross a busy street in a German city. My German associate was standing next to me. As soon as I saw a break in the oncoming traffic, I began walking toward the other side .. and as I recall, I wasn't right at the corner, either. Right away, he grabbed my arm and acted horrified that I would do such a thing. Not only that, but someone on the other side actually shook a finger at me!*
>
> Service project management, USA/Germany

The business areas most affected by this dimension are contracts and agreements and how or when they should be modified. Some executives and professionals are firm in the belief that only their own laws and procedures are logical and effective:

And this senior vice president came down here and thought he was going to do business like the Americans do—and he wanted to change the whole country. That's the main reason he failed. He told everyone [exactly what steps he was going to take] and the mayor called me and said "What's going on here? I can cancel this any time I want!" We had to basically remove him from the region. It was impossible to do business with him.

Environmental management, Latin America/USA

There are a certain number of (American) companies, if they've never done business abroad, they think they can just cut a deal the same way they do in America. Or, they've got a formula that works in Asia and they think they can just duplicate it all over the world. The answer is, no. That's naive.

Consulting and law, Czech Republic

In countries with a "one-size-fits-all" outlook, a contract is carved in stone and trustworthy associates abide by it to the letter. Lawyers hammer out the details, signatures are affixed, and it's a done deal forever. Elsewhere, contracts may be viewed as subject to change according to circumstances, and business associates should be willing to honor the need to adapt to changing business conditions. This process is summed up by an internationalist:

It took us almost a year to develop a twenty-page contract. The basis was what we used in the U.S. and presented to the client. They just refused—said "We don't like this." They wrote their own contract. Then it was a chance to get them both together and produce the third version, which was the sum of the two. Now we have a model that can be used with minor modifications from here on. It's a piece of art because it satisfies both sides. But it took a year.

Water quality and wastewater treatment project, USA/Brazil.

Greasing the wheels

In some societies, it's understood that rules are necessary, but they need to be adapted to fit individual circumstances. This flexibility is the basis for many misunderstandings about what constitutes corruption—a huge issue for Western business. In many places, gifts and favors are considered a regular part of business dealings, and calling this "corruption" or "bribery" produces great confusion. It's simply the way things are done. Without these gifts and favors, business deals are stalled, supplies may not be delivered, or critical stamps of approval are not given. The following excerpt illustrates how uncomfortable it can be for an expatriate to adapt to such a context, even when he succeeds:

> *I had a big problem justifying certain business expenses. How do you submit an expense report to corporate accounting saying that you spent $50 as a "gift" so you could get a telephone? I had a choice. I could give the $50 or wait at least a year for a telephone. What would you do? You negotiate an up-front sum from your company to do what needs to be done, and don't ask me how.*
>
> Anonymous

U.S. laws forbid companies to offer these kinds of "gifts." The Foreign Corrupt Practices Act bars all American citizens and corporations from offering money or anything of value, directly or indirectly, to any foreign government officer or official that is not due in the normal course of activities. (The lack of a receipt, or an official's unwillingness to provide one, may be an indication that an unethical demand has been made, and therefore one is in violation of the law.) The intent, of course, is to halt the practice and spread of bribery and corruption. However, in the opinions of some internationalists I spoke with, the rigid enforcement of this law by corporation management has had a negative impact on the competitive position of some U.S. firms, and has not, in fact, completely prevented the practice.

World opinion and business practices are gradually changing in the matter of greasing palms. Bribery and corruption are less and less accepted in business as it becomes clear how seriously they discourage business investment in developing nations by promoting cynicism and distrust. (The problems of rampant bribery and corruption are discussed in more detail in the section on the former USSR at the end of this chapter.) Anticorruption agencies are now being established the world over.[5] Nonetheless, internationalists must be prepared to recognize and contend with the practice and expectation of gifts and favors in certain parts of the world, especially in developing areas where the practices have been in place for years.

Concept of time

Anthropologist Edward T. Hall's in-depth study of time and how various cultures determine and relate to it provides the foundation for an understanding of this dilemma.[6] He uses the term "monochronic societies" to refer to cultures where people do one thing at a time, scheduling events as separate items. In contrast are "polychronic societies" in which many things can be done at once. This contrast defines one of the most challenging of all business issues, and one over which people expressed frustration time and again during my interviews.

The timeline (monochronic)

In many Western cultures people perceive time as proceeding in a straight line; an event has sequential segments—a beginning, a middle, and an end. Things are organized around time, task, and place. Idiomatically, time is "saved," "wasted," "lost," or "used wisely" like money or electric power. Management terms like "critical path," "deadlines," "completion goals," "time-sensitive," and "time-critical" occur in every meeting. Productivity and production are measured, and faster is better. Time is money, and punctuality is exceedingly important.

The time spiral (polychronic)

In some other societies, time swirls through past, present, future in continuous motion, and elements of one can be mingled in another: past in present, future in past. Because time is perceived as flowing continuously, the ways people respond to it are flexible and ever-changing. Time is organized around people. Roles and responsibilities may be undefined and changeable. Many things can be done simultaneously, or things can be done in more than one way. Time is an environment, not a resource.

This can be disconcerting to people used to linear time perception:

> *The organization had no structure. It was like a soccer team of six-year-olds. Someone kicked the ball and they all ran to one side of the field. The ball was kicked again, and they all ran back in the other direction.*
>
> Mining, USA/Latin America

Spontaneity is important in the polychronic society. Many things may interrupt deadlines and schedules; for instance, project specifications may be revised to improve quality or design, even if deadlines have to be set aside to do it. Appointments may be canceled or delayed to meet the needs of friends or family. Meeting times are approximate. Planning might be done by determining a goal, then arranging and rearranging the methods of getting there. Business is accomplished through relationships with people and completing transactions rather than through slavish adherence to predetermined schedules and timelines.

> *Flexibility is so important. We call it in Portuguese "jogo de cintura." It means literally "loose in the waist" and it means a relaxed attitude. You need to be able to move according to the situation—dance according to the music. And to be able to not only see it but to take advantage of it.*
>
> Environmental project, Brazil/USA

> *My area is India and Malaysia. Here it takes longer to accomplish things because the infrastructure often isn't there. The phones don't work, you don't know if the electricity will be cut off. And people have the sense that even if*

you have a fixed deadline, if you can get around it, then it's
okay. It's not that bad to miss a deadline because time is sort
of a nebulous concept that you see not only in business situ-
ations. People invariably come in late.

Food products manufacture and distribution, Malaysia

We call it rubber time here, because it stretches.

Consultant, Malaysia

The second comment above reflects the fact that where infrastructure is undependable, people are likely to adapt to that fact by
"loosening" their own time behavior—an exercise that most internationalists will be required to perform.

Communication styles: How we say what we say

Language is one of the fundamental elements of a culture. On
a superficial level, people have difficulty in other cultures because
they don't command the vocabulary and grammar of the local
language. Yet there is much more to communication than this:

The western mode of communicating is verbally—we
don't put much emphasis on nonverbal. I worked many
years in Indonesia as an employee who happened to be
foreign. We had a two-hour program for trainees coming
from all over Indonesia about the meaning of "yes,"
because it can be said or implied in many many ways, and
people from the different islands didn't necessarily under-
stand the meaning. It's not obvious for everybody. It's very,
very subtle.

Business development, Denmark/Indonesia

Just consider the physical variables of a communicative
encounter. The speakers choose to sit or stand a certain distance
apart. They touch each other to emphasize their message, or they
refrain from touching. They look each other in the eye or avert their
gaze. They gesture or remain still. Their voices may be loud or soft,

varied in pitch or monotone. They interrupt each other or wait politely for replies. And no matter where they come from, all humans perform some variation of all these things simultaneously and usually without reflection, whenever they talk.

All these behaviors have meaning. They serve as signals directing the conversation, letting the listeners know what the speaker is trying to accomplish and how he expects the listeners to contribute to that goal. The problem for internationalists is that different cultures perceive the same signals in different ways.

Take something as simple as a pause during speech. Researchers have found that people are keenly aware, to a degree of fractions of a second, of how long a speaker pauses between statements. When the pause exceeds a certain length, the hearer assumes that the speaker is finished talking for the moment, and expects a reply—that is, the speaker is finished with his "turn." The catch is that different cultures employ different rules. American English speakers expect shorter pauses than do people from some other groups; as a result, they may hear a "turn-ending" pause and start to talk before their foreign partner is through with his statement. This error in turn-taking is then perceived as a rude interruption. In a reversal of this situation, some cultures (for example, Caribbean Spanish speakers) use simultaneous speech— talking over the top of their partner—as a form of positive feedback: "I hear what you're saying and I'm helping advance the conversation." Anglos, however, are likely to perceive simulta- neous speech as rude.

Popular awareness of communicative differences has been growing in the past decade or so. The discoveries linguists have made by comparing different cultures, age groups, and even genders are becoming available as practical guidelines for people who want to communicate more effectively. Seminars on cross- cultural communication can be invaluable for anyone going inter- national, and they are enjoyable, too: anyone who talks can relate to discussions of communication.

Communicative style is often a large element in the stereo- types people form of other cultures. For instance, North Americans and northern Europeans are regarded as "unemotional" because

The Internationalists

they tend not to vary the pitch and loudness of their speech much, and they don't use expansive gestures; Latin Americans and Latin Europeans are "demonstrative" or even "passionate" because these features are more marked in their conversational style. Of course, there is a range of individual variation in every population, but there is also a typical norm, and this behavior is learned as one grows up.

The highly adaptable internationalists can often respond intuitively to different communicative strategies and even start imitating them effectively. Virtually all areas of business are affected by different methods of verbal expression, but the particularly problematic areas are:

- negotiating style
- team behavior
- management style

Communicative display, which English speakers often call "expressiveness," runs the gamut from poker-faced neutrality to extravagant arm-waving, hand gestures, loudness, and pitch changes in voice. People accustomed to restrained, quiet conversation may overinterpret an emotional response, assuming that the other person is angry or upset. In fact, that level of expressiveness may be perfectly normal in the other's culture. (If you've observed the misunderstandings in American families that blend different cultures—say German and Italian—you have probably seen good examples of this, and even laughed about them.)

You have to follow up closely and you have to work with people here more than in the U.S. They are emotional.
Industrial products manufacturing, USA /Brazil

Likewise, the use of silence is keyed to cultural standards. In Western cultures, people often feel uncomfortable enduring an extended period of silence during a meeting or social interaction. Indeed, they may feel compelled to offer some comment simply to fill the empty space. Their foreign associates, however, may perceive silence as thoughtful and harmonious, and constant talk as intrusive, loud, unnecessary, and thoughtless.

Friendliness, nurturance, understanding, and harmony are seen as polite characteristics in some cultures, but other cultures may regard such behavior as soft or weak.

Achievement, drive toward accomplishment of work goals, and focus on performance are all hallmarks of an assertive culture in which people express themselves strongly and willingly offer opinions. However, people from countries that value modesty and politeness may see these characteristics as heavy-handedness, arrogance, and unwillingness to compromise.

Body language

Some say that as much as 70 percent of our face-to-face communications are accomplished silently. Spending just a few hours in a country where a different language is spoken will rapidly reveal just how significant it is. When the verbal component is impossible, the only way to get the idea across is to point, wave, mime, or make faces. As you might expect, this sometimes has humorous, even downright funny results. I recall, for example a situation in which my friend and colleague resorted to sneezing at a sales clerk in a Ukrainian grocery store to indicate that she wanted to buy pepper. Or the giggling Japanese drugstore clerk who placed product after product in front of my suffering husband, who was desperately trying to describe an upset stomach and a head cold.

Body language can also include such conscious and unconscious variables as the distance people stand from each other, the firmness and duration of a handshake, hugging, back-slapping, or kissing, and the meaning and length of eye contact. It also includes body posture (both standing and sitting), how the limbs are positioned (close to or away from the body), facial expression, hand gestures, and so on. Clothing, jewelry, and grooming accentuate the messages we send with our bodies.

All humans quickly form judgments about people and situations based on their own cultural programming, by using nonverbal cues, sometimes unconsciously and within seconds. But it can be dangerous to a relationship to apply culturally determined standards outside your own country. I've seen an unsuspecting Western man react with horror when kissed on both cheeks by an effusive European!

Many people (especially some Asians) have developed a high degree of skill in "reading" body language:

> *I remember thinking after a while how thirsty I was. Within minutes, my Korean host had quietly placed a cup of tea beside me on the table. I had not said a word. She just knew. That kind of thing happened regularly.*
>
> Education, USA/Korea

Around the world, hand and body signals have different meanings. Anyone attempting to establish rapport and build a working business relationship who ignores these silent messages is asking for trouble. Excellent books, videos, and trainers are available to educate travelers and businesspeople in the cultural details of body talk. Common sense dictates that people educate themselves so they will not misunderstand or offend their foreign partners.

When cues are missing

Talking on the telephone in a second language is a challenge that brings home the importance of the nonverbal elements of communication. Have you ever tried to telephone for hotel or restaurant reservations in a foreign country? When you can't see your conversational partner, it's much more difficult to interpret meaning. E-mail is yet another realm where the significance of these signals is obvious. It's terribly easy to be misunderstood or to give offense unwittingly in terse written correspondence fired off on the spur of the moment. When the recipients can't see you, the softening influence of a smile or a touch is not available.

The complications of nonverbal communication in cross-border business are compounded by advances in technology, which have increased the speed at which information is exchanged and business is done, but at the same time have created a whole new range of human interaction problems. Teleconferences, faxes, e-mail and virtual meetings inject challenges in such areas as written expressions and graphics, in addition to the misunderstandings that are a regular part of written communication between people with different levels of language fluency. It's much easier to misunderstand when people are not face to face. There is no way to "read" the nonverbal signals that comprise, some say, up to 70 percent of communication. Cryptic e-mail messages leave little time for the relationship-building or social interaction that are so vital in many parts of the world.

Get to the point

"Context" in communication is the sum total of what you have to know in order to communicate effectively: the information, attitudes, and understandings that are shared by the parties to a conversation. In cultures described as "high-context," messages are likely to contain a great deal of implicit meaning. Language may be metaphoric or poetic; messages may be embedded in stories. In high-context cultures, people may not state a point quickly, but rather talk around it or refer to it obliquely. They gather much information from the environment or from observing others. There is a rich and subtle tangle of relationships and traditions that is difficult for outsiders to penetrate.

> *"We share the same light beneath the sun and the moon." The president of the Japanese company always spoke so poetically.*
>
> Manufacturing, USA/Japan.

> *The concept of privacy is nonexistent in a collective, "we" culture. Here, you have to poke your nose into other people's affairs. So you grow with that kind of sensitivity, where someone is in bad shape, he or she doesn't have to articulate it. You just know. You pick up the vibrations.*
>
> Human resources, Malaysia

In "low-context" cultures, by contrast, information is stated explicitly and in detail. High-velocity messages are delivered directly and often bluntly—as easily observed during any television commercial break in the Western world. People from high-context cultures may interpret this communicative style as a lack of sensitivity or subtlety:

> *Americans only know what they read.*
>
> Resources exploration, Southeast Asia

Unlearning—and Relearning

The dilemmas that originate with cultural differences cause endless problems, and subsequent delays, in cross-border business. With the examples related by my interviewees, I hope you have begun to realize how your own culture has stamped the way you deal with your world, its organizations, and its people. Simply understanding that you are culturally programmed is only the first stage. As curious as it may seem, it is not an easy task to identify one's own cultural imprints. We have become what we are very slowly and almost unconsciously. Cultural learning, or imprinting, begins in infancy. Throughout our lives we are conditioned by our societies, our schools, our government, our professions, and our organizations. Employees learn early in their tenure with a company that they either must conform to "the way we do things here" or leave. We have all been boxed by our respective cultures, to the point where the box has become invisible to us. But it is certainly visible to those from other parts of the world.

Bringing together people from different countries and different organizations who have been imprinted by very different cultures will assuredly cause a cultural clash. Often, simply being ourselves can create problems. This is especially true when a businessperson has had little or no contact with other cultures and expects everyone to behave the same way or to have the same understanding of their tasks and goals. Contrary to what many of us heard while we were growing up, people are *not* pretty much the same everywhere. It's time to begin to unlearn.

Metaphorically, unlearning can be likened to digging up last year's plants from a vegetable garden so new ones can be planted, or sanding the old varnish off a table so a new finish can be applied. It's about emptying something or cleaning something out, making an opening and creating an opportunity for something new to come in.

Titan Wang, the thoughtful managing director of AC Nielson in Taipei, told me a Chinese tale that illustrated this point perfectly. He had been talking about the difficult changes his own organization experienced after the merger of two companies and the associated management and culture shifts.

There was a great master who wanted to learn something from a greater master, so he went to him and hoped that they could meet. He was kept waiting in the guest room for three days, and he kept asking when it could be arranged. Just wait, he was told. He will meet with you. Finally, on the fourth day, they said, you can come now. So he went to see the greater master who asked him to hold a bowl, an ancient Chinese bowl. An empty bowl. And then the greater master poured water into this bowl. The water filled the bowl and began to run out, but he kept pouring until the pot was empty. Then he just went away. The one holding the pot didn't understand. The next day, the greater master called for him and said, "Do you understand what I am trying to tell you?"

"No," said the great master, "please enlighten me."

"You are just like that bowl—full of water. There is no room in your life that I can teach you anything. So you must empty yourself first." [7]

Wang went on to say that this story was an important one to him because it illustrated the need to create some space for new things, new ways, and new knowledge.

The Internationalists

Author Danah Zohar expresses it this way:

> *Rewiring (the brain) means making the effort of decon-*
> *structing (tearing out) all the old connections as well as*
> *laying down new ones. We resist it. So long as no great*
> *challenge rocks the boat, we resist spending energy we*
> *could save. But if things have gone badly wrong in our lives,*
> *if our original mental and emotional habits and our deeply*
> *held assumptions can no longer cope with some new*
> *challenge or experience, we HAVE to rewire, or go under.[8]*

Expressed as a challenge, this means suspending judgment about rightness and wrongness; it means questioning the origin of our feelings of frustration, anger, or lack of control in a business situation. A new position that is in conflict with an old position will seem wrong, unless the old one is first suspended. Comparing "our" way to "their" way will continue to keep cross-border business collaborators apart by supporting the division of "us versus them."

With the great variety of challenges and differences to deal with, it's obvious that mistakes will be made. Unintentional faux pas and hurt feelings are bound to happen, even in the most well-considered international projects and by the most astute and intuitive of internationalists. I heard often that these events are usually understood and forgiven when "intention" is present. That means the clear, obvious intention of team leaders and members to try to do the right thing. Dealing with differences in team members isn't a case of defining who is right and who is wrong. Differences are—just differences. Intention will go a long way toward building a climate of understanding and a functional multicultural team.

Countries and Satellites of the Former Soviet Union

The field issues that are intensified and complicated by cultural factors are universal in that they exist to varying degrees in most of the world. In the former Soviet Union and its satellites, there are unique issues that are so significant that, for the time being, they overshadow everything else in the socio-economic environment. Because this part of the world is so different from anywhere else, I have elected to devote a separate section to its circumstances as they relate to business practices and behaviors of people involved in business ventures.

Little if any empirical research exists for cultural comparison of this part of the world with others. The economic conditions that are a result of decades of a command economy have so altered the cultural programming of the people that this region is radically different from most other parts of the world.

In the winter of 1998 I had the opportunity live and work in Ukraine. Until then I hadn't truly appreciated the devastation wrought by the years of communism and its subsequent downfall. The former Soviet Union is a massive world region experiencing cataclysmic culture shock. The struggles are profound and on a scale that has dramatic impact on these countries' organizations and smaller work units. The Central European countries of Poland, Hungary, and the Czech Republic are much farther along in their business evolution, probably because of their past identification with the West, their greater industrialization, and their shorter history under communist domination. Their economies are rapidly improving, with investment and privatization efforts on a large scale. The situation is different in other parts of the former Soviet empire. One interviewee spoke of the countries east of Central Europe as "the Wild East."

The move from a command economy to a market economy has thrust an entire population into a state of confusion. Some results of that massive culture shift that directly impact business are highlighted below.

1. *People don't clearly understand the purpose of business.* The question "Why are you in business?" is likely to produce the answer, "For the people who work here." Profit is a brand new idea, and to many it is a principle that is somehow suspect.

The Internationalists

2.   *The consumer sector is undeveloped.* There is little under-
     standing of the concept of consumer, or customer.
     Moreover, there is little understanding of the importance of
     product quality or customer service.

3.   *There is little knowledge or understanding of commercial
     processes in the rest of the world,* although there is great
     curiosity. Some areas have immature, untested, or
     constantly changing commercial codes which can be
     subject to political pressure and corruption.

4.   *There has been no experience with the concepts of personal
     choice, initiative, and accountability,* which dramatically
     affect the implementation and operations of business
     projects.

Because no substantive body of empirical research is yet
available that compares the behaviors of people in the former
Soviet countries with others, the information here is based on my
personal experiences and the observations and experiences of
others who have worked there.

Historical perspective

For decades the people have been controlled in their commercial—and indeed personal— lives. They were told where to study,
what to study, where to work, and where to live. In factories and
offices, their work and professional lives were dictated. There was
no free market to influence the demand for or production of goods
and services. Nearly every facet of people's lives was controlled by
the state.

This is painfully obvious when one wanders the streets and
stores of cities in parts of the former USSR. Store windows are
sparsely furnished with dusty products; shelves and counters are
arranged with no thought to attractive presentation. There is clearly
no sense of merchandising; a bizarre hodgepodge of wares are
stacked in unimaginative arrangements. In some cities, the old

Soviet-style stores are still prevalent. Customers must wait in line for the attention of an uninterested clerk. Products are warehoused behind counters and cases and must be handed to a requesting customer for approval. Guards and store "traffic cops" are posted everywhere to keep an eye on everyone.

This extreme level of control has also devastated the social environment, which today is characterized by the absence of trust, sense of community, or an ability to self-actualize. Many people simply have no idea what to do with themselves. They have been abandoned by a system which made their decisions and took care of their basic needs.

Another issue that was mentioned during interviews in this part of the world was that of ethnicity. Because much of the region has been part of a centuries-long geopolitical tug-of-war, borders have been redrawn, ethnic populations have moved back and forth, and generations of people have survived wars, purges, and conquerors. Today ethnic Ukrainians live in Romania, Hungarians in Bulgaria, and Poles in Latvia. The conflicts in the former Yugoslavia and other parts of the Balkans are bleak testimony to the depth of discord when fiercely proud ethnic populations live outside the current geographical boundaries of their majority groups. With the tyrannical control of communist regimes removed, age-old ethnic conflicts reassert themselves. These volatile ethnic frictions can significantly affect the ability of business groups to function.

What does this mean to Western businesses entering these markets? First, the potential markets are huge and the opportunity enormous. So are the risks for the unwary and unprepared. Any business venture into these markets deserves extremely careful study to assess the political, legal, and financial risks. Second, the operational end of the business will assuredly present special human challenges in selecting and developing partners and teams.

The way it is

The first thing is that whatever they want to do, it's going to take a lot longer and it's going to be a lot more complicated than they think. And it'll be more expensive. There is a much higher cost of setting up business and getting it going. The second thing that is shocking is that information is hard to come by here. It doesn't seem like it should be, but it is. There's not a lot of information that people are used to providing and they like to keep it secret. That's left over from the old regime. So in terms of being well informed as a business person, it's very difficult. Another thing is that there are really good, smart people here, but they haven't had a lot of experience and they need a lot of hand-holding. That's part of what takes time and costs money, but if you are a manager or an owner coming over here, your investment can't just be your money. It has to be your time. You can't have a passive investment here. Unless you've got a good project manager on the ground, it's not going to work.

Diane Holt, Attorney; CEAG, Prague, Czech Republic[9]

People in this part of the world are generally highly literate, intelligent, and well educated. This region was, after all, a superpower. Many of them possess formidable technical and scientific skills. That is not the problem. The problem is that there is only minimal understanding of market economics. Business venturers must plan to devote time to business education, getting down to things as basic as "Why are we here?" "What is the purpose of this business?" and "What is a customer?"

Here are some principles I have heard from people with experience:

Don't hire anyone over the age of thirty-five—maybe even thirty.

I cannot attribute this quote to anyone specifically, because I heard it from nearly every person who has done business there. It's appalling to write off an entire generation or two of potential workers, but the communist society left many of the older generations without the ability to make decisions or take initiative with regard to their professional lives. Many find it impossible to deal with the huge changes in philosophy and practices that have swept their country. Unless they are told precisely what to do and when to do it, they simply do nothing. Many younger people have a more flexible and far-reaching grasp of the world and are more open to new ideas and methods. I'm sure there are exceptions to this rather frightening state of affairs, but comments like this were too numerous to ignore.

Teamwork is not something that this crew understood. They came to me to ask about every little thing. I have to say all the time to take some initiative—to use your own judgment. It's a struggle.

This remark was made by a young Western-educated manager with a young staff. I got to know this group personally and found them extremely energetic and willing—but they had been together for nearly two years. Part of his solution has been to make each person responsible for a particular area of work, have them coordinate their respective pieces with each other, and provide them with training by experienced business people at every possible opportunity.

You are going to have to put in the time and attention to develop your partners.

Spending the time to build relationships is as important here as in other parts of the world. But in former Soviet countries, it goes beyond simple relationship-building. It also means figuring out who needs to learn what, and then making sure that happens.

My work experience convinced me that the people are smart and curious; they are accustomed to studying and learning, and they are good at it. The problems are not with the people's willingness but with the political and systemic chaos that historically and currently surrounds them and frustrates their desire to use and develop their individual abilities.

No discussion of this part of the world would be complete without addressing the issue of corruption and crime. Since the implosion of Russia in 1998, the situation in that country has deteriorated to near-disastrous levels. Other countries of the former Soviet bloc, with the exception of the more westernized central European countries of Poland, Hungary, and the Czech Republic, are also in the throes of corruption, though perhaps not to the extreme degree found in Russia. The U.S. Embassy in Moscow is cautioning businesses to hire reputable security services because extortion and corruption are common in Russian business. Organized criminal groups target foreign businesses and demand protection money under threats of violence. Bribe-taking is widespread throughout the Russian bureaucracy.

Despite these challenges, many foreign companies already there intend to remain, as evidenced by a recent American Chamber of Commerce in Russia survey of 101 companies of various sizes that currently do business there.[10] Virtually all areas of their business operations have been affected, and yet they seem to feel that they are in it for the long term, and that the difficulties of waiting out the current economic crisis will be outweighed by the potential within the next decade.

Transparency International, a Berlin-based nongovernmental organization fighting corruption, published its 1998 Corruption Perception Index for 85 countries. The findings are based on the perceptions of businesspeople, risk analysts, and the general public. On the bottom of the scale can be found Romania (number 63), Bulgaria (66), Ukraine (71), and Russia (76). Only some African countries fared worse.[11]

The myriad cultural, economic, and political issues are of critical significance in this part of the world, and confronting them will be a formidable task for any internationalist. In addition to learning about the very different cultures from country to country, and how they have been altered by seventy years of communist domination, people working there will also have to be concerned about corruption, crime, and possible ethnic conflicts, as well as educating their staff in the most basic areas of Western-style business. Then they will have to devote consistent time to building a working environment of trust that will allow fundamental changes to take place. (For an example, see chapter 4, case studies on Russia Telecommunication Development Corporation and on Kabelkom.)

Summary

Culture and its manifestations are very real conditions that affect business dealings everywhere in the world. Culture is a system of shared understandings that is transmitted among members of a group, whether organizational or national/regional. These two divisions are further divided into smaller cultural layers. Internationalists universally commented on the need for foreign businesspeople to understand the culture, values, and traditions as well as the business and legal systems within a country. The major dimensions of difference that can cause conflict are the practices involving relationships between people, the differences in the concept of time, and wide variations in communication styles, both verbal and nonverbal.

Internationalists and others in the global game must practice "unlearning" in order to make way for different ways of thinking and behaving. What is real or right in one culture may be completely different in another. Differences are neither right nor wrong—they are simply differences. The internationalist characteristics are absolutely vital to business relationships.

The former Soviet Union is one area of the world where exceptionally difficult conditions exist. Decades of communist domination have left a dramatic cultural stamp on a population that today is surviving in chaos. Businesspeople entering that market will be challenged in a number of ways from financial and legal standpoints, and most markedly in the attitudes and behaviors of a population that is unfamiliar with the concepts of initiative and choice. A long-term command economy has radically affected their ability to understand the concepts or market economics and business in the Western sense. A substantial commitment in terms of education and trust-building will be required.

4

Internationalists and Their Stories

In the following accounts, selected from a number of conversations with internationalists in several countries, people talk candidly about their experiences. The cases profiled represent a cross-section of industries in world regions both turbulent and dynamic. These include Latin America, Southeast Asia, Eastern Europe, and Russia, as well as fully industrialized countries with sophisticated international dealings. They demonstrate a variety of circumstances in which these internationalists use their special combination of characteristics: tolerance, flexibility, curiosity, and the ability to deal with ambiguity. The cases also reflect a variety of organizational situations, including internal corporate enterprises, joint ventures with numerous partners, consultant-led projects, and organizational blends.

Collecting the interviews was an education in the realities of cross-border dealings. The knowledge I gathered through first-hand research was an invaluable resource. Theory became reality. No two people presented the same scenario. Each experience was different, with its own collection of issues based on the internationalists themselves, the industries concerned, the countries in which the business took place, and the cultures—both organizational and native—of the project participants. Their experiences speak for themselves.

Product Development : Becton-Dickinson, biomedical and clinical diagnostics

What you gotta do is, you gotta listen.

—Doug Kawahara, interviewed in 1997

Becton-Dickinson and Company, a $2.8-billion multinational biomedical company, is engaged in research and development as well as the production and distribution of medical and research products through its many international subsidiaries. Doug Kawahara, the project co-leader for one specific product-development effort, is a fourth-generation Japanese-American with formidable educational credentials and a quiet, confident manner. He described the project and the product development team—a group of people from two world regions, but working within the same division of the company.

The objective of our division's business was to develop a new integrated platform for performing histopathologic tests. In other words, examining biological materials on a slide and analyzing the expressions of different markers. My role was to help coordinate the efforts among reagent people who understood the biology and/or histochemistry and how to make the assay work appropriately, and software and hardware people who knew electronics and optics and how to control instrument components and to make them work together. In addition, the software people needed to understand what needed to be analyzed from the perspective of the reagent people. The reagent and software and hardware people had to be working together.

The team was created with people from the Netherlands and the United States. Kawahara talked about the challenges of getting these highly-trained, individualistic scientific and technical specialists working together while simultaneously dealing with the cultural differences:

> *Americans tend to be a lot more flexible in how they look at things; their perspective can change depending on need. I think we found the Dutch to be very precise and exacting and when they analyzed something, what they concluded or decided could become the only acceptable way to go. The challenge was to make use of their precision and yet get a little flex to make some modifications that were needed. Even within the U.S. team, we had a certain amount of cultural differences with people born and raised in different parts of the world but integrated for many years into the U.S.A. Certain tendencies came up where an individual would say, "Well, the boss said something and that's right," even if they technically thought he might not be.*

One challenge that emerged early in the team experience had to do with technical language. It became obvious early on that the different technical specialties, each with its own jargon, were using identical words to mean different things. Kawahara used the word "application" as an example:

> *One group would think about an application and to them it meant putting reagents on a slide and having a certain reaction that you could measure. The software team, however, thought about application as a combination of certain tools within a given software package that were not specific for a particular end result.*

It was soon clear that they would have to define a common language. Kawahara added that he didn't think it was absolutely necessary to get to complete agreement on everything—just to get to a point where everyone worked together to achieve a common goal. He thought that formal work on team development process early in the life of the team could have short-circuited a lot of later problems.

Kawahara and the team co-leader, a Dutch scientist, were selected for different reasons. Kawahara was chosen because of his scientific background, coupled with an understanding of strategic planning and business development. His Dutch counterpart was selected because of her technical and project management skills and because she had been the head of the R&D team in the Netherlands and knew their capabilities. Neither was selected for anything other than technical or business skills.

Fortunately, however, Kawahara possesses a strong ability to deal effectively in ambiguous situations and to manage disparate groups with flexibility and sensitivity. This project greatly enhanced his ability to operate as an internationalist and gave him a new understanding of the skills needed to be successful in that arena—skills he greatly values and feels he will use continuously in the future.

Product Development

Name: Douglas Kawahara

Company: Becton-Dickinson and Company, biomedical and clinical diagnostics, $2.8 billion annual revenues

Position: Director, Reagent Development Applications

Project and purpose: R&D team, product development. Develop integrated platform for performing specialized pathologic tests.

Team members: Netherlands, United States

Challenges: Bringing together people with very different perspectives on work. Some with biology/chemical orientation, some mechanical/optical and some software. Developing a common language as well as dealing with cultural differences. Flexibility in work processes was a continuing issue that we never overcame. Some were willing to reconsider processes and try a new way. Others were committed to continuing the old way.

Do differently? Start earlier for team unity. Get them together early in the process so more planning happens jointly.

Advice: Make sure you get enough knowledge of differences in work style. A clear understanding of objectives is critical. You can't throw people together and expect immediate cooperation. Establish ground rules and make sure everyone understands that we are mutually dependent upon each other for success.

Joint Venture: GTECH do Brazil, services to national and state lotteries in Brazil

Do it GLOCALLY: define strategies in a global way but apply them in a local way.

— Antonio-Carlos Rocha, interviewed in 1997

This project began as a joint venture between the American corporation GTECH and Brazilian Racimec. Racimec, now a division of GTECH, has been awarded the contracts to provide computer technology and consulting to national and state lotteries in Brazil. The parent company, GTECH, is a $730-million organization servicing 75 lotteries worldwide. Company president Antonio-Carlos Rocha talked about the management team he put in place when he was hired to build the company in Brazil. Initially, he says, there was a very poor relationship between Racimec and GTECH.

So I came in to make the transition between the Portuguese of Racimec and the English of GTECH. From a team formation standpoint, I had to start from scratch. And the one thing I wanted to do, and I did, was to create a team from completely different company cultures. What I looked for was diversity.

Rocha believes that diversity is critical to the success of teams. He explains that he means diversity of corporate backgrounds:

I brought in a guy from IBM, another from Citibank, a guy from H-P, and a guy from a family-oriented Brazilian company who had worked in a multinational American environment. They were all Brazilian, one a Japanese-Brazilian and one female. I didn't bring in anyone that I knew. I wanted to start fresh and build a culture here. GTECH doesn't have a strong corporate culture itself. It's a young company, fifteen years old and not very big or very

*internationalized—not a lot of policies and procedures. It's
very entrepreneurial, projects and goals oriented without a
whole lot of bureaucracy. So it's not a traditional company
at all. There isn't really a culture to import.*

Rocha continued, explaining why he thinks it's important to
assure diversity in a team:

"It's crucial in terms of starting something new that you
have different opinions coming from different cultural backgrounds as much as you can." He quoted an article that identified
the success factors of a company: customer intimacy; product
leadership; and operational excellence. He said, "You have to
have two of these three to be a success. If you have only one, you
may do well but you're not going to be a leader in the marketplace." The management team he assembled were individuals
who came from companies he says exhibit at least two of these
success factors.

Together, the management team built a working relationship,
bid on the contract for the national lottery, and won. Rocha said that
today the company's relationship with the customer is excellent.
Operationally, they are right on target. The third success factor,
product leadership, is a challenge, because product leadership
assumes that competition exists for the business. In this case, the
company has won the contract to provide the services to the sole
customer, so there is no competition. They do it all.

Rocha, however, is determined to ensure product leadership, so he is creating competition for himself. He has created a
second company to service the state lottery of São Paulo and
formed a holding company to regulate the two. These companies
will compete against each other and set the stage for product
leadership.

A savvy businessman, Rocha talked about difficulties putting
an effective team together:

*More and more I am learning to select people and build
teams based upon their true motivations. You have to be fast
today. Look for excellence—but don't look forever. You have*

to move—you can't wait for 100 percent perfect. Reality isn't 100 percent perfect.

The company has secured long-term contracts, but Rocha takes nothing for granted. He continues to work on customer intimacy because his customer is the government, and he knows very well that governments and government officials change, as he says, "faster than private businesses."

Joint Venture

Name: Antonio-Carlos Rocha

Company: GTECH do Brazil—originally a joint venture
                     between Racimec and GTECH, Inc.

Position: President

Project and   Joint venture, now a business unit of GTECH, Inc.
purpose: Provide software and consulting services to national
                     and state lotteries in Brazil.

Team members: Brazilian

Challenges: Start from scratch and build a team from diverse
                     corporate backgrounds.

Do differently?   I wouldn't hire a guy from IBM—at least, not the
                     old IBM. Maybe the new.

Advice: Make sure the team shares a common vision. It's
                     something that is rational, but it is also emotional.
                     Passion, intensity that you put in what you do is
                     very critical to success. They must be connected to
                     what they are doing, have a reason to be a part of
                     the team and believe in that reason.

Joint Venture: Santa Elina Mines, gold mining

To rebel against discomfort is to rebel against change.
Discomfort creates stimulation.
— Bob Armstrong, interviewed in 1997

Santa Elina Mines was a company formed through a direct investment by U.S.-based, Canadian-owned Echo Bay Mines in the Brazilian company Santa Elina. The management team of the new company was comprised of two Canadians, one American, and seven Brazilian managers from their respective organizations. The president and CEO, Canadian Bob Armstrong, was the only Echo Bay expatriate in the Brazilian operation, living and working at Santa Elina's headquarters in São Paulo. The other North American team members commuted regularly. A thoughtful man, Armstrong talked about the challenges he faced in blending the two very different organizations into a new entity:

> *Echo Bay did an initial foray into Brazil, and this was the biggest venture the company has attempted. Echo Bay had for the most part no international experience, so from that aspect it was interesting to set the stage with Brazilians who also had no international experience. This was the first attempt by both companies going international. A transition team was established by Echo Bay to come down and help transition this essentially Brazilian company into an international organization. The team was established, work plans were set up—all in North American style. Ninety-nine percent of the plans were done by North Americans.*

Armstrong talked about the things that were done right and those that were not. At the beginning of the project, a training company was hired to provide the team members with information and acculturation in the behaviors and cultural differences they were likely to encounter. This was valuable. However, the Americans and Brazilians were given the training separately; the two were never brought together prior to the initiation of the

venture. He thought this should have been done: "As a conse-
quence, things were left undone from both sides. The team never
fully closed." He went on:

> *The actual transition ...when I went there ...the Brazil-*
> *ians said the Americans didn't practice what the training*
> *company had preached. They said, "You people operated*
> *too fast and all you did was demand information and you*
> *didn't let us contribute first. When we asked for informa-*
> *tion, we didn't get anything back. It was very one-sided."*
> *On the other hand, the Echo Bay people were concerned*
> *because they thought the Brazilians were hiding informa-*
> *tion. What I found is that there is a period of trust-building,*
> *a period of establishing within the country.*

Armstrong used the drawing shown in Figure 4 to illustrate
what he meant. He described the blocks as "cells of excellence, or
cells of knowledge. They are groups of people, but the glue—the
glue in the team is trust and communications." He characterized the
glue as that mortar between the blocks that cemented the individual
cells together as a unit.

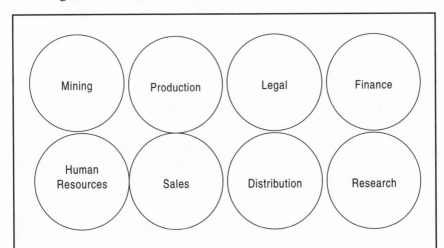

Figure 4. Cells of Excellence. *The management areas of an inter-*
national mining company.

Santa Elina Mines overcame its initial barriers to communication. Armstrong said:

> *Fifty percent of our meetings became instructional.*
> *Either they instructed us or we instructed them. And we*
> *discussed concepts like this, about what was going to make*
> *the company work. We couldn't do it without them and they*
> *couldn't do it without us. If we were going to do this, we had*
> *to have the glue. We had great people—now we had to do it*
> *together. So we sat and talked about getting things up on the*
> *table—nothing hidden. And it took a long time. They always*
> *called us "the guys from Echo Bay" and we called them*
> *"the guys from Santa Elina." People's minds were separate.*
> *It took me about three months to realize this and to figure*
> *out how to get the message across. If I go international*
> *again, I'll do it within a day.*

Armstrong said the two biggest challenges in starting an international joint venture are cultural orientation and public vs. private
company backgrounds. The Brazilian company was a traditional
Latin organization: privately held, patriarchal, with employees
promised employment for life. The Canadian/American organization was a public company with the North American values of
technical competence, quick response, productivity, and strong, no-
nonsense work ethic. Because Brazil had been a closed economy
for the seventeen years preceding this venture, it had developed its
own way of doing things. Introducing international work practices
and standards took a lot of instruction and sensitivity, but to trade
on the international market, Brazilians had to learn what the international community wanted and needed. The two issues, cultural
and organizational, were equally time-consuming.

After several months of struggle, the team began to solidify.
They faced external business challenges, but as a unit, they began
to work. Armstrong said it took constant attention to both organizational and cultural differences. They continued to work at trust-
building and communication—the glue that bound them together.

Echo Bay ceased its participation in the project in mid-1998 as a result of an abrupt drop in the price of gold. This event triggered a reorganization and corporate downsizing across the board. At the same time, the executive group went through significant changes, reorganizing the priorities of the company. The Brazilian partner also suffered with the drop in gold prices and has been unable to carry on with the projects, although it has retained the rights to them.

Joint Venture

Name: Robert C. Armstrong

Company: Santa Elina Mines, a $200-million joint venture
                   between Echo Bay Mines (Canada/United States)
                   and Santa Elina Mines (Brazil)

Position: President and CEO

Project and   Direct investment in existing Brazilian mining
purpose: company for exploration and mining of gold.

Team members: Brazil, United States, Canada

Challenges: Bring American know-how and competence into the
                   Brazilian organization. Build trust and communica-
                   tion between two very different organizations and
                   cultures.

Do differently? Bring the teams together at the beginning to
                   establish common vision and provide training in
                   working together.

Advice: Begin the first day to make the new organization
                   into one unit—not the separate organizations from
                   which they came.

Privatization Venture: Telefónica de Argentina, telephone service in southern Argentina

You can't live with somebody you always think is wrong.
—Eduardo Caride, interviewed in 1997

Telefónica, one of two Argentine telephone companies, was owned and operated by the state until 1990. The privatization operation was engineered by a venture among three groups: Citibank of Argentina; Telefónica de España, the Spanish telephone company; and Techint, an Argentine economic group. The three formed a company, Cointel, to take the state-owned telephone monopoly private. It was a mammoth undertaking. A company executive, Eduardo Caride, the director of area residential communications, who was instrumental in the privatization, talked about the process:

> *We did this takeover, approximately 300 people working during six months in advance, to analyze everything. The team was approximately 25 people from Citibank, 70 Spanish, and 200 from Techint. Each group had a leader that was responsible for the project. It was very difficult because we had four different cultures—the three companies plus the [existing telephone company] of 21,000. This was the startup and there were a lot of conflicts—basically coming from the different cultures of each of the companies.*

He described the cultures. Citibank, he says, has basically the same culture worldwide; he describes it as "American." The Spanish telephone company was European in nature, and Techint was Argentine.

> *There were several challenges. The first one was to get one common vision. Each of these three had different cultures, or ways to do things. The first challenge was how to blend the differences, because each was pushing the company in a different direction.*

Caride talked about the difficulties that project leaders from different organizations had in communicating their progress back to respective company heads. They had to go back to their constituencies and support or defend deals to their bosses. People from outside the team hampered its functioning by making demands on the team leaders. This, he thinks, is a major cause of problems in international projects. He says it causes a lot of fights and lost time because the project leaders must then go back into the team and renegotiate. He emphasized that it is critical to be absolutely clear about what is to happen and who is in charge:

> *When you have three companies that have put a lot into the transaction, the three of them saying that the deal is [bad] and each one deciding how to do this and how to do that—well, you just need a unified decision.*

He added that it's critical to have more than two partners. With three, two of the partners can persuade a third to a course of action or break a tie. With only two, it's impossible to get a decision made if they disagree.

Because this project was so complex, unified vision followed by consensus on next steps was absolutely essential. Huge changes were made quickly. The leadership team led the organization through reductions from 21,000 employees to the current 12,000. Caride talked about other changes that were implemented over a four- to five-year period at a cost of $5 billion:

> *The first things we did were very easy because everything was a mess. For example, we had almost 5 percent of the [telephone] lines out of order at the time of takeover. A phone line used to cost $5000 and you bought it on the black market. People used to wait five or six years for a line from the phone company. When you sold an apartment, there was a price with or without a telephone—a $5000 difference. There were a lot of things to do and we did them. We built a network, shaped commercial offices, put uniforms on employees. It cost a lot, but it was easy to*

decide what to do. Now the rest, what we have to do now is much more difficult. I say it this way: we changed the hardware. Now we have to change the software. It's what the people have in their minds. Changing the software is much more difficult and it doesn't have the same type of impact as the things we did before.

He was talking about changing the culture of the company to focus on customer loyalty and to become a competitive organization.

This team, which is now merged into the new company, led the new Telefónica de Argentina from a state-owned monopoly to a private business and now into worldwide competition, within a ten-year period. It served as the leading case—the model—for the privatization of state-owned monopolies in Argentina.

Privatization

Name: Eduardo Caride

Company: Telefónica de Argentina, provider of telephone and related services in southern Argentina. Net income, 385 million pesos.

Position: Director of Area Residential Communications

Project and purpose: To privatize the state-owned telephone monopoly in Argentina.

Team members: Argentina, Spain. Team members from consortium of three participating companies.

Challenges: To keep the team together. Three companies with a lot of doubts were in a very risky situation. Then, to establish and keep a common vision.

Do Differently? Be very, very clear who is boss. You need unified decisions.

Advice: Know your partners. Understand the logic and rationale of the other cultures. Then, you either accept it or you find another partner.

Joint Venture: Samsonite, manufacture, marketing and distribution of luggage

Don't pretend to know it all, even if you're top dog. That's why we build teams.

—Jim Peters, interviewed in 1997

Samsonite, one of the best-known luggage manufacturers in the world, today employs more than 10,000 people around the world. Its products are distributed throughout five continents, producing $800 million in revenues. Jim Peters, retired senior vice president and president of Samsonite's international group, talked about his team experience directing the start-up of the company's manufacturing operation in Italy. A Yugoslavian by birth, he grew up and started his career in Europe. When he began with Samsonite, managing the European operations out of Belgium, the total volume of business was $7 million. When he left fifteen years later, it was more than $200 million in Europe alone. A true internationalist as a result of both upbringing and experience, Peters brought to Samsonite considerable sensitivity to cultural issues, both personal and organizational.

We had a distributorship relationship in Italy which was not satisfactory. So we needed to move from one distributor to another, and at the same time we felt we needed some manufacturing to take place in Italy because of styling, of the ideas people had there which were more advanced than ours. The idea was to use Italian talent for innovation and styling and satisfy the marketing of that country. At the same time, we wanted to design products which would be interesting elsewhere as well.

Peters described his approach to getting the Italian team operating with the American company:

Samsonite had a 60/40 partnership. We said the Italian manager knew what he was doing, so we weren't

*going to interfere in their way of doing business or try to
impose on them some marketing philosophy. We had some
manufacturing assistance from our Belgian factories,
where we had the center for European production.
Basically, we observed in amazement how well they did.
The Italian managers and their dealers were very close, a
family relationship with lots of togetherness. We could not
reproduce this—it was so Italian. We were not going to
interfere.*

He talked about the personal relationship he developed with
the Italian family who ran the factory—a relationship that became
a deep friendship in time. He said this type of relationship can pay
off handsomely for teams entering a new market, if they are willing
to invest the time and energy to cultivate the relationship on several
levels. He emphasized that both parties benefit in these relationships if they genuinely try to help each other and not take
advantage. It's a bond of trust and respect.

Peters's success in Europe earned him the spot as head of
Samsonite's international operations, where he led successful
teams in other parts of the world, including such diverse cultures as
Mexico and Japan. Everywhere he worked, he spent time and effort
cultivating and nurturing personal relationships with in-country
businesspeople. He says:

*The most important factor (to success in a country) was
always to try to understand with whom you are dealing. I
always liked to develop myself. I would never go to a
country without knowing their history, and political
situation at the moment. And I was genuinely interested.
Sometimes I was accused in a friendly way of being too
interested in local politics and so on. And yes, when I was
in [these countries] I wanted to know all about them. It
helped because you don't do business just in the office. You
go to dinner. You meet a family. And what do you talk
about? You can't talk about baseball, because they don't
know what it is. You talk about things that they are inter-*

ested in. This worked everywhere. They appreciated my interest and understanding of their background.

As much as Peters advocates letting capable foreign partners run their own operations, he cautions that the company interests must be balanced. The perspective of the parent company is very important. He thinks this is best done by putting in place a local management team that includes a parent-company representative.

Selection of team members for Samsonite's international ventures began at corporate headquarters with an established international group of experts in manufacturing and finance. When they needed different skills and knowledge, they drew on the domestic operation. Peters said they specifically selected people who were recognized for tact and understanding:

We selected first by the skills they had and then by knowing and talking to them. We tried to develop these people for future use in international affairs. It was a kind of recruitment and training as we went along—a seasoning.

Peters's experiences were broader than most because of his lengthy career. His business success is proven. His wisdom, gained from worldwide experience, is rooted in respect, trust and a genuine and personal interest in his business partners.

Joint Venture

Name: James S. Peters

Company: Samsonite, luggage manufacturer; $800 million
                   annual revenues

Position: Senior Vice President of International Operations
                   (retired)

Project and   Joint venture to manufacture, market and distribute
purpose: Italian-designed high-style softside luggage in
                   Europe.

Team members: Italy, United States

Challenges: The team was made up of technicians, marketing,
                   manufacturing and finance people. The group had
                   to be conditioned to operate internationally, to
                   understand how to handle other people—and to do
                   this without interfering with their individual
                   technical knowledge.

Do differently? I was accused of being too soft, too nice with
                   people. But on the positive side, I always had
                   excellent results.

Advice: Don't reinvent the wheel. Point out advantages of
                   working together. Pick the best features from the
                   group. Break the barriers of local pride and
                   jealousy. Discuss. Exchange experiences.

Joint Venture: Kabelkom, first pay movie channel in Hungary

*Most of my success overseas has been because I have
taken the time to befriend the local people that I work with.*
Linda Sweeney, interviewed in 1997

Kabelkom is a complicated joint venture of HBO, Time-Warner, Time-Warner International, TCI Cable, US West, and United International Holdings. This complex project was conceived by a Hungarian-American executive from one of the large American partners who assembled the joint venture group for both financial and strategic purposes. Collectively, they spent $30 million acquiring various ownership positions in nine Hungarian cable systems; then they launched a Hungarian-language version of HBO.

Linda Sweeney, the chief financial officer for the project, now pursues an interesting and challenging career as a contract professional, working on long-term temporary assignments in various parts of the world in startup television ventures. A twenty-year veteran of the television business, Sweeney earned an MBA from Harvard University. Her role in Kabelkom lasted about two years. She talked about the issues and challenges faced by companies entering markets that were formerly part of the Soviet bloc, as they begin to embrace a market economy.

*It was in 1991-92, just about the time the country was
coming out of their Iron Curtain shell, so there were a lot of
problems, banking issues, legal issues—but also the
cultural aspect of people for the first time trying to learn
about business and how to make a profit and how to work
efficiently on a day-to-day basis, accomplish goals and take
responsibility for getting the right things done, rather than
just blindly following detailed orders.*

The project was overseen by a ten-member board of directors representing the six American companies that met monthly by conference call. None of the directors was in-country, except for the

part-time CEO. Sweeney and nine other Americans ran the project
in Hungary, with a staff of 40 local employees. The complexities of
the organizational structure and the challenges of building a
working team were evident from the beginning, since the members
came from different organizations and served different masters:

> *Five of us came from HBO, the rest from various cable
> television entities around the U.S. So we had the New York
> programming people, the Denver and Southern cable TV
> people. That in itself was a cultural clash.*
>
> *What they failed to take into account was not only that
> this was the first international joint venture for most of the
> partners, but it was the first in Eastern Europe for all the
> partners, and at a very strange time for those countries.
> They just did not have the mechanisms in place that you
> would take for granted in a normal business situation. We
> didn't have the ability to get enough local currency or hard
> currency to do daily tasks, or even the ability to get
> telephone lines. We had about 50 people in our office and
> we had five phone lines that would just routinely stop
> working. So you'd be in a conversation, talking on, and the
> line would just go dead. You couldn't get office supplies, file
> folders—you just had to spend an inordinate amount of time
> trying to get the basic stuff done. You couldn't get
> computers. I had a new dishwasher in my apartment, but I
> had to go to Austria to buy dishwashing detergent.*

The original plan was to have the expatriates in place for a
year or two. They would train their Hungarian replacements who
would take over, and then the partner companies would lose the
expense of maintaining the expatriates. Seven years later, however,
they still had three or four Americans there, all of them second-
generation expatriates. Sweeney thinks the original business
planners were naive in their expectations regarding both budget and
timing; they did not understand the length of time it would take to
get a team fully assembled and everything in place given the pre-
existing conditions.

So most of the people there were just bleary-eyed trying to get everything done, and everybody was all stressed out. The reality is, though, that it's usually impossible to [have everything in place] in international ventures. To meet political commitments or other deadlines, you often have to start operations missing key staff. It's hard to recruit all the right people quickly for these jobs.

You start out saying what you used to say in New York, "Yes, I can get that done ... no problem." But you don't often have the resources in place to do it well. The challenge is to manage their expectations without having the board think that the problem is your lack of management skill!

Sweeney went on to talk about fundamental problems that the planners didn't consider—problems that are rarely thought of in advance:

I would say that at least half your time, at least in the first year you're involved, is just trying to live. Trying to get by. Trying to do the tasks that you would take for granted, that you would turn and have an assistant do. Well, suppose you can't find an assistant, or they don't speak English, or they've never had to answer a phone before. They don't know how to take a message, they don't understand that when you're in a meeting and you can't be disturbed, you really don't want to be disturbed. They probably never worked on a computer. You have to train them. So rather than turning to an assistant and being able to off-load certain tasks, it almost doubles the time since you have to train them to do it before you can give it to them.

She hastened to say that this isn't a failing on the indigenous staff's part, but rather a basic difference in the way things are done:

There are always going to be intercultural differences in how they feel they need to do the job well. The level of supervision that they want, or the level of supervision that they expect, is going to be different from what you've been used to. In most of the countries I've dealt with, both Soviet and non-, the people that are working for you generally are used to a very detailed level of supervision and they have never in their lives been rewarded for any initiative in going beyond that. You have to sit down and in a very patient and supportive manner, spell out exactly what you want, and exactly how far they're supposed to go and then you have to keep checking back to make sure that they're doing it, as well as positively reinforcing their attempts to use their judgment. And it's not that they're lazy, it's just that they're not used to being allowed to take any more initiative than that. Of course, this takes a lot of your time, but showing your frustration just makes things worse.

She continued musing about the project elements, theorizing:

U.S. companies can afford to have high standards because they have the resources to invest and the tools to accomplish them. In developing countries, they define "success" and "quality" at more modest levels, appropriate to the resources they have available. Our local employees thought we were crazy to insist on quality levels they had never seen before. Our customers had no point of reference beyond the other television channels and systems they had seen locally. So, we were killing ourselves to satisfy the wrong audience.

Despite all the complexities of this project, from an organizational perspective as well as from the cultural and logistical issues of doing business in an emerging Eastern European economy, Sweeney says that the project was successful:

Everything eventually worked there. The goals were eventually met. It just took longer. And I think the realization of that, that everything was going to be fine, finally hit everybody. But unfortunately we made ourselves crazy for many months and that was mostly unnecessary. The team aspect ... finally worked by the time I left because everybody finally realized we were dependent on each other. That interdependency worked but it took a long time before we got it.

She agreed that some kind of team development in advance of the project would have been extremely valuable, especially in gaining consensus and developing the leadership.

Sweeney talked thoughtfully about the value of learning about and appreciating new ways of working, and of developing lasting relationships in other cultures:

I remember, I was reading a book at that time which had been translated into Hungarian—it was an American novel—and this cashier who worked for me was reading the same book. Without speaking too much we were able to convey how much we were both enjoying the book. It's so important to take that time—and it's so nice. It's a part of working overseas that I really like—that human interaction that is prized much more than it is here in the U.S. Here we're much more businesslike. Frankly, one of the nicest things about working internationally for me is that I get to experience the different cultures. It's nice sometimes that different cultures don't work on weekends and they spend time with their families. Maybe it means they don't get as much work done, but they have the richness of living with their family in that leisure time that we don't prize as much. I came back a much better person, more balanced, more effective, and definitely more humble. I don't think I will ever again make the mistake of working seven days a week, no matter how busy we are. You lose too much perspective, begin to work hard rather than smart, and most importantly, you lose a part of your life.

With the Kabelkom project behind her, Sweeney continued her international contract work with projects in South America and Australia. She was in New York at the time of our interview, working on a new project for another former Soviet state, this time in Central Asia. "Having lived through a particularly difficult start-up, I specialize in plugging the holes while the permanent team is being assembled," she concluded.

Joint Venture

Name: Linda Sweeney

Company: KABELKOM, a joint venture among HBO, Time-Warner, Time-Warner International, TCI Cable, US West, United International Holdings, and nine Hungarian cable television stations

Position: Chief Financial Officer

Project and purpose: Joint venture to provide HBO in Hungarian, the first paid movie channel in Hungary

Team members: Hungary, United States

Challenges: Americans, both in-country and back in the U.S., expecting the same level of detail and precision that you would expect if you were doing something in the U.S. It was humanly impossible, given the circumstances we were working under.

Do differently?   Start earlier to insist we had realistic budgets, enough people to get everything accomplished. Then you don't have to deliver on unrealistic expectations.

Advice: Take time to get to know the people, to build the relationships with your group, to build a level of trust. They will be less likely to test you all the time and more willing to help you.

The Internationalists

Joint Venture: Hua Mei Confectionery Company, Ltd. (Sino-American Confectionery Company), manufacturing bubble gum, chewing gum and candy products in China

Get the people pulse.

—Virginia P'an, interviewed in 1997

"It's a good thing I was much younger then. I probably grew a lot of gray hair during that period," said Transcapital Group Chairman Virginia P'an of this joint venture project that she and her company were hired to develop and manage, as she says, "soup to nuts." "Now I'm known as the lady who brought bubble gum to China."

The venture began as an idea by the CEO of the Finnish confectionery manufacturer Huhtamäki Oy, which then owned Leaf North America (now owned by Hershey) and produced consumer confectionery products (such as candy and gum). He hired P'an to go to China and find out whether the Chinese would be interested in developing a confectionery business. With an impressive background in international banking and many solid business relationships in Asia, she was a logical choice. Born in Chongqiang, in Sichuan province of China, she emigrated with her professional family at an early age. An instinctive internationalist, she made a name for herself as a pioneer, overcoming barriers against her youth, ethnicity, and gender to rise steadily in position and influence, first at the Federal Reserve Bank in New York and later with American Express Bank in Asia.

In 1986 P'an made an exploratory market feasibility trip on behalf of Huhtamäki and Leaf to probe the Chinese market and study the people, the economy, and the Chinese government's interest in developing the domestic consumer market in the confectionery sector. Fluent in nine Chinese dialects, she found it relatively simple to assess the business possibilities. The product had been successful in other developing countries because it was easily affordable (its price can be pegged to the local currency) and it provided enjoyment to many. Her research was conducted on the streets, in taxis, and in stores, talking to people in everyday situations. She strongly believes in the hands-on approach to market research, calling it "taking the pulse of the people." She also uncovered a huge piece of market intelligence: bubble gum was actually in the Chinese government's five-year food plan.

After that assessment, which clearly signaled opportunity, P'an took the news to the Finnish CEO, who excitedly gave the go-ahead, seeing that their product was a hot prospect in a huge market. He sent P'an to conduct a market-entry survey to find out how to set up the venture, identify prospective partners and factories, and then interview all the appropriate people. She assessed transportation issues and population base as well as facilities. The site she chose was Wuxi, a pleasant town about 60 miles from Shanghai, known affectionately as "Little Shanghai." Then she assembled the team.

The Finnish CEO assigned a board member of the North American Leaf group to work with P'an. Together, they brought in a German engineering team and an American law firm, selecting the members for their technical expertise and management talent. The American lawyers were chosen because they had knowledge of the Chinese language and laws, both written and spoken, as well as English. In China, only contracts written in Chinese are binding; their English versions are not.

The German engineer was recruited "because he had done a number of factory setups in third-world countries and was familiar with the systems that don't work—so he knew how to make them work. And he was a real people person. But more important, he was very technically competent. It's not like building a factory in the U.S. or Western Europe; a lot of things you have to make do. You have to be entrepreneurial."

Flexibility, cultural adaptability and patience to explain and to teach were other major selection criteria for team members.

The challenges became apparent immediately. Doing business in a country that had been politically and economically isolated from the rest of the world for fifty years was not for the faint-hearted. The group had to know the Chinese joint venture laws, which were new at the time, and help local authorities interpret them so the business could be approved.

P'an explained how they established a joint venture company in China with a Western management team. The first general manager was an Irishman, recruited by Huhtamäki and Leaf, then interviewed by P'an and the others on the team to make sure he had critical skills. They then identified the first local management team, all Chinese:

> *We basically had to train all the local Chinese, and some were very stubborn. You had to come at them from all different ways. I mean, you really had to explain your concepts in many different ways. And when you didn't get across with that, then you had to get all the people around that one person to agree with you, and you gang up on them.*

All joint ventures in China are done with an existing company or with a local government entity. So they began with a Chinese company and westernized it. All business concepts were unfamiliar in this newly opened country, and no one had experience running a company like a Western enterprise. They began early on to select staff members with an attitude that supported a profit-making, commercial enterprise. Then they provided both functional and management training for the management group and the local workers.

P'an remarked on the length of time it took to accomplish their business goals. She said the Finnish CEO understood the difficulties:

> *The Finnish people are very strong and very spirited. They've been doing business with Russia for many years and things don't get done quickly there. So they didn't have a glamorous idea about going to China. Given the nature of the company and the CEO, we decided we'd take a different approach. Usually, people sell a project based on unrealistic expectations. What we did was double the amount of*

time we thought it would take, for all the uncertainties. We figured it was better to say three years, and come in at two or two and a half, rather than have the company cripple through, then have to go back to the board and say we need another half million for this project because these are all the things that happened we didn't anticipate.

After deciding that it should take one and one-half years, they doubled that estimate. In fact, the project was brought to completion, with the factory up and running and almost the entire town of Wuxi trained, in two and one-half years.

This factory has since become the most successful joint venture in Wuxi. The products are widely known throughout China. The factory has been expanded five times since the completion of the original project in 1988.

Joint Venture

Name: Virginia P'an

Company: Hua Mei Confectionery Company, a joint venture led by Huhtamäki Oy, a Finnish confectionery company

Position: Chairman, Transcapital Group, consulting company facilitating the joint venture.

Project and purpose: Joint venture to introduce, manufacture, and market confectionery products in China.

Team members: United States, China, Finland, Germany

Challenges: Getting the Chinese to understand. Taking them from early nineteenth century to late 1980s thinking. And keeping the Western side and the Chinese side in sync.

Do differently? I would have charged my client a lot more for blood, sweat, tears and hardship!

Advice: Learn as much as you can about the market you're going into. Learn the culture, the history, and the people's hot buttons. Do your own market research.

Joint Stock Companies: Russia Telecommunication Development Corporation, telephone service

Be a welcome guest.

— Victor Pavlenko, interviewed in 1998

"It was wild and woolly then — and it's still wild and woolly today since the system of laws is evolving slowly. It's a fascinating place, Russia. They say there are laws and regulations, but relatively speaking, there aren't," said Victor Pavlenko, talking about his experiences leading the holding company formed by telecommunications giant US West to make investments in regional joint ventures for telephone switching and cellular service in post-Soviet Russia.

Pavlenko had spent several years in and around Eastern Europe and Russia putting together startup joint ventures for US West. In 1992, when US West decided to increase investment in Russia and create an operating company to direct their anticipated telecommunications investments there, Pavlenko, his wife, and their two dogs packed up and moved to Moscow. Over the next few years, he and his team structured complex financing agreements, built joint stock companies, managed political intricacies, developed strategy, put operations staff in place, and solved the myriad problems that arose in a complicated economy marked by rapid political change and deteriorating social and economic conditions.

Beginning at age four, Pavlenko has spent most of his life tramping around the world. Born in the United States, he was educated in Australia and Switzerland, and combines a widely diverse business background with an internationalist mindset. Prior to joining US West, he had been a minister, an educator, and director of a nonprofit organization. He joined the company during the wide-open telecommunications race generated by the breakup of the Bells in 1983-1984. His job ultimately became investment resource allocation, or looking at international operations for investment potential.

Pavlenko talked about his experiences with the series of joint ventures that spanned Russia from Moscow to Irkutsk, a city in Russia's remote East on the shores of Lake Baikal, near the

Mongolian and Chinese borders. He reflected on the way it was and the way it is now:

> *I learned that historically business got done in the Soviet period through negotiating agreements with govern-ment ministers. If you had an agreement signed by a minister, you were 90 percent of the way to the bank. Then the Soviet empire sort of imploded. Decentralization occurred overnight and regions of Russia and the former republics were suddenly in charge of their own futures.*

He went on to describe the intricacies of the wheeling and dealing that went on at various levels in the new Russian bureau-cracies:

> *So now if you're a governor of a region in Russia and you have economic development as a priority, you know you need to have an effective telecommunications infrastructure in your region as a precondition to that economic develop-ment. In the old days, in the centrally planned economy, you got the money for infrastructure from Moscow. Moscow wants taxes today, but the planned investment loop back to the regions doesn't work. So you say, I'm not gonna give Moscow anything; I need to keep all the tax receipts in my region. So governors want improved communications infra-structure and they want it today. They don't want to wait until tomorrow when the federal government has communi-cations network standards, national development plans, and so on.*

He explained why they focused their joint venture efforts on a regional rather than national level:

> *The thing I learned was you had to do these with common sense, with people of good will that you came to trust. There are some of those in Russia—we had some really great partners. The one in Irkutsk was terrific.*

Pavlenko talked at length about the difficulties he faced in finding willing experts who would move from the US West fourteen-state North American region to Russia to take over management of the ventures. He said the perception of living conditions there made it impossible for him to recruit appropriate in-house talent, even though his efforts were supported by top management who considered the Russian ventures very important. People simply refused to go.

> *So, we just opened the door and got a couple of recruiting firms and we recruited people from outside US West. I kept my fingers crossed. We put in Portuguese, we put in Australians, we put in Canadians. I interviewed every one of them.*

The Russians had insisted that the managing director in each of the joint venture companies be Russian. However, although the Russians were very capable operationally, they did not have the business experience to manage the ventures, so foreign expertise was critical:

> *There was nobody, virtually nobody, within Russian telecom to start this up and really grow it. This is an entrepreneurial undertaking. Most of the Russian entrepreneurs were not available to us by then— they were off doing other businesses and got their start in '88 or '89. The Russian personnel we did hire didn't understand the kind of accounting we needed done: the technology, marketing, sales. And it wasn't because they were stupid. They just didn't have the background and experience. It didn't exist in Russia.*

The short-term solution was to put someone in the managing director slot who was politically savvy—a consummate diplomat. Then they structured the next level with a couple of expatriates with management and business skills and filled in the rest with Russians having the requisite technical skills.

Pavlenko interviewed every potential manager himself. One of his major interests was cross-cultural capability. He described his litmus test as follows:

> *If you were out in Russia somewhere, you have your family with you, and you or anyone of your family need emergency medical care, would you accept it from Russian healthcare providers? And if they said no, they were done. There has to be a sense of equality to start with. They can't be talking down.*

It was clear that not everything could be run by expatriates. They were expensive as well as hard to find. The Russians involved in joint ventures were well aware of the expense of these foreign managers, but they also knew they couldn't run these telecom businesses alone. Pavlenko said they understood the problems in exactly the same way: How were they to structure the organizations and populate the management levels to keep pace with the growth trajectory of the business?

They began to move some Russian talent from Moscow and St. Petersburg, but that became a challenge in itself because Russians are much less mobile than non-Russians. It became as complicated as bringing in expatriates, since to enable the Russians to move, the company had to deal with housing, travel for families, and other benefits. The heads of the regional joint ventures, along with Pavlenko, pondered. Business training was required, but on such a scale that to implement it themselves would be to kiss profits good-bye.

The long-term solution was far-reaching. In 1989 Pavlenko had designed a business skills training program that was piloted in Hungary. They exported it to Russia in 1995 with a $14 million investment from USAID and investments from other Western companies. They also opened the highly successful Center for Business Skills Development, which graduated 2,000 students in its first year. It has since spread geographically and has been taken over by Thunderbird School of Management, after a competitive scramble by big U.S. universities to operate it. The core curriculum is simple and basic: business systems, functional specialties like accounting, human resources, sales, and marketing. All courses are designed to train people to a task. The idea was not to graduate MBAs but to provide the basic business skills that Russians lacked and to give all companies coming into Russia a cadre of people trained in Western-style business basics. Even after the radical changes in Russia in late 1998, the Center for Business Skills Development continues to function profitably, despite the financial crisis. It remains an important institution for basic business skills training as Russia struggles to find a way through its present situation.

Pavlenko says about this project, "It was really a way of building something that was bigger than we could ever or would ever have done alone, by understanding that we all (Western companies and Russians) had similar problems, and by leveraging." He admitted, however,

> *If I was going to do it today, though, I'd do it differently. What is absolutely clear today, this is not a free-market economy and it won't be in the short run. It's basically an oligopoly, a series of cartels. And that shouldn't be shocking because that's the way it's been run for years. If you understand [that this is not an emerging market economy with competition], you do things differently.*

Pavlenko strongly believes that doing it the Russian way is the better choice for businesses. He talked about the fact that, as an example, Russia has not adopted different accounting standards; thus joint ventures with U.S. partners are required to keep two sets of books—one for the partner, and one for the Russians. And it is the Russian version that really drives the business, because it is constructed to deal with the local tax situation.

Pavlenko also said he would rather not have brought in so many expatriates, although the ones they had were smart, energetic, and enthusiastic. "They were young, and we wound up training the expatriates and the Russians at the same time." He believes that the business should have been "Russified" early by bringing on

Russian equity partners at the holding company level, giving them the support they needed by acting as technical and professional consultants, and then allowing them to develop in their own way. "The people who I think have been most successful in Russia, have enabled Russian-style operations," he said.

He continued, talking about attitude and how much it means to business ventures everywhere:

> *I want to spend much of my time being a tourist and learning. I like music, art, history, military history. I've never been to a place I didn't like. The partners [in Russia] began to figure this out and started arranging events that allowed them to show their pride, their full history and culture and help me learn and enjoy.*

Pavlenko talked about the difficulties he observed other companies experiencing in Russia and his assessment of their corporate attitudes, and how that resonated in the post-Soviet economic era:

> *Remember, these are superpower people. They are used to setting things up and having these things go the way they want. If you want to bring capital and some technical know-how and learn from us and be a humble guest, then you are welcome and we will be good friends for a long time. But if you don't approach it that way, you're done. There are a lot of stranded foreign assets in Russia today—people who went in there with the kind of mind-set that said, by God we won the cold war and you people are headed for a demo-cratic free market capitalist economy, and we're here to lead the way.*

Until the Russian economic meltdown in the late summer of 1998, the ventures were doing just what they were supposed to be doing: growing. Since then, however, the entire telecommunica-tions industry, along with many others, has been virtually destroyed, wrecked by a government that defaulted not only on external creditors but on its citizens too. Although emergency measures were taken to preserve the continuation of service, rapid depreciation of the ruble and the banking crisis played havoc with the industry as a whole and resulted in a revenue reduction in cellular service of 40 to 50 percent in three months.

Joint Stock Companies

Name: Victor Pavlenko

Company: Russia Telecommunication Development Corpora-
                 tion, a holding company owned by US West Inter-
                 national and seven outside investors

Position: President and CEO

Project and   Investments in start-up Russian telecommunications
purpose: companies

Team members: Russia, United States, Canada, United Kingdom,
                 Ireland, Portugal, Croatia, Scotland, Ukraine,
                 Armenia, Azerbaijan, Pakistan, India, Australia, New
                 Zealand

Challenges: Missed expectations relative to laws and regulations
                 for conduct of business. Both sides underestimated
                 the size of the task. Second, finding, training, and
                 retaining personnel to manage and operate the joint
                 stock companies with rapid growth rates.

Do differently? I would have "Russified" it earlier and used expatri-
                 ates in the holding company as de facto consultants
                 to the local operating personnel in the regional
                 joint stock companies.

Advice: Be a welcome guest! For me, it's not a chorus, it's
                 an attitude. You sit over coffee on the street, go out
                 and ramble about, just sort of see what's there. If
                 you're putting in a communications network, you're
                 involved with how people communicate and
                 interact. You must understand something about the
                 culture and behavior.

5

Internationalization Solutions:
Tactics and Tools

This chapter addresses the human side of internationalizing companies. It presents specific processes and tools to establish and maintain an environment and culture that are "internationalist friendly." Simply speaking, that means a top-down understanding and appreciation of what it takes for individuals to be successful internationally, coupled with organizational policies and practices that recognize, support, and develop internationalists.

It is relatively easy to apply Band-Aid remedies here and there as problems show up during the course of an international project. It is an entirely different matter to undertake a large-scale initiative on an organizationwide basis. In a company that sees itself as global, this means developing a culture that embraces a worldwide perspective. It means implementing globalizing practices inside the organization, then linking these to globalizing tactics in field projects by providing appropriate tools that will boost internationalists' success.

As I analyzed the thoughts and suggestions of the interviewees, one thing became increasingly clear. To internationalize a company, its executives and leaders must themselves understand and appreciate at first hand what it takes to be an internationalist. That means they must travel: not on overseas golf vacations or corporate junkets, but rather in a thoughtfully planned program of internationalization that incorporates experiences intended to provide specific exposure to international business situations and people. In plain language, it is essential that executives, leaders, and managers get their fingers in the global soil.

This, of course, costs money, and most companies attempt to save money in areas they consider "noncritical." Many corporations I've encountered tend to save by cutting travel budgets, along with training budgets, as a way to rein in escalating expenses. That defeats the whole purpose of this hands-on approach.

Neither I nor any of my interviewees advocate lavish corporate jaunts. Quite the contrary. Travel for the purpose of internationalization should be undertaken strategically and within established budgetary guidelines. It needs to be planned as part of a larger internationalization initiative. It can be coupled with specific practical learning programs to encourage active involvement in internationalizing the overall mindset and practices of the company and its vital human capital.

As my interviewees expressed their thoughts about what business leaders and their employees need to know and do to become internationalized, a pattern of strategies and tactics began to form. This pattern of solutions mirrored the problems they identified, as related in chapter 1: the ideas fell into groups at the organizational level and at the project level. Figure 5 depicts this array of solutions; some are mine and some are aggregates of suggestions from others. Of course, not all of these will be appropriate for every company. Variables of size, industry, timing, budget, and stage of corporate development will affect the usefulness and implementability of these tools. Common sense will dictate which are most usable.

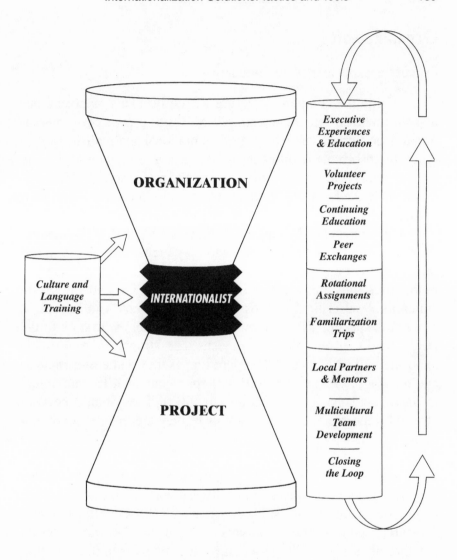

Figure 5. *Tools for internationalization at the organization and project levels.*

Organization Level

Executive experiences and education

Within the company structure, executives have opportunities to gain practical experience simply by visiting their own international operations. Site visits provide a practical and realistic opportunity to absorb the realities of daily life in a foreign environment. The advantages are dual: leaders learn "the real story," and internationalists in the field stay in touch and build relationships with their corporate leaders.

Unfortunately, this approach may not be met with standing ovations from those in the field, who may view a site visit as interference in their ongoing activities. It must be carefully set up so that both sides buy into the mutual benefits. The all-important "intention," so critical in cross-cultural situations, can become a powerful aspect of the process. Corporate leaders who go into the field should ensure that their visits are structured to provide exposure to the realities of the operation; as they gather information and receive briefings, field staff will appreciate their leaders' intent to understand the local situation's realities. They should be very clear with the project leaders they visit: they are there to learn, not to audit or take over.

Another method is the experiential business educational program, where executives from different parts of the world come together to share visions, solve problems, and cross-pollinate ideas. Executive educational programs offered to the public bring together people from different companies and parts of the world; in the same way, a large international company can bring together its executives from different divisions and locations.

Public international executive educational programs are becoming more plentiful. Some excellent ones exist under the umbrellas of recognized international academic institutions. Notably, INSEAD in Fontainebleau, France, and the American Graduate School of International Management (Thunderbird) in Phoenix, Arizona, offer creative, thoughtful programs for the international executive. Harvard University's Program for Global Leadership offers both campus-style learning and opportunities for on-the-job activity. Numerous other programs are available at sites worldwide. Many of these programs are offered as custom-designed units of varied lengths for specific organizations or industries. They are increasingly attracting attendees from all over the world, providing unparalleled opportunities for interaction and relationship-building among executives worldwide.

Exchange opportunities can be found through professional associations that attract executive membership, through chambers of commerce, or through service-based organizations. For example, Rotary International sponsors Group Study Exchange, a business-oriented team exchange program operating throughout the world. It is also possible for corporations to sponsor their own exchange programs, which can be structured to fit specific needs.

Executives tend to be isolated by their positions, and so may be unwilling or unable to participate in educational or training opportunities available to other members of their organization. But because these leaders are so vital to the vision and mission of the organization as a whole, it is critical that they experience the internationalizing effect of dialogue and interaction with people from other parts of their world.

Volunteer projects

Volunteering abroad can provide profoundly internationalizing experiences. Volunteers have the chance to live and work with individuals and businesses in developing areas of the world and to share their expertise in very concrete ways. It's an unparalleled opportunity to gather some real-life understanding of cultural and economic issues in places where Western companies will be developing new markets. It's also an exciting opportunity to build solid relationships with businesspeople and potential partners in emerging markets.

Volunteer projects may last only one or two weeks, or may involve longer commitments. Usually, all or most of the volunteer's expenses are paid by the sponsoring organization. Some of these organizations, such as IESC (International Executive Service Corps) and CDC (Citizens Democracy Corps), receive funds from USAID. They cover the map in terms of their needs for industrial and functional expertise. The two mentioned here have web pages that give detail about their mission and projects. Find them at www.iesc.org and www.cdc.org, respectively. Other international volunteer projects are often sponsored by service-oriented not-for-profit organizations, or by churches and other religious organizations.

Companies can get a lot of mileage out of volunteer projects. Executives and managers gain international experience; companies gain significant public relations value in new markets; and the project affords an unmatchable "look-see" opportunity. Most of all, there is enormous satisfaction in making a personal contribution in places where the need is greatest.

Continuing education

Companies of all sizes have instituted schemes of tuition reimbursement or financing for degree programs. Some companies even bring college classes in-house, affording opportunities to study in a corporate setting. When corporations acknowledge the value of internationalists, there will be an increasing number of working and professional-level students who need courses and degree programs that prepare people for this kind of career.

Degree programs or college studies aren't the only way to provide internationalist educational opportunities to employees. There are many cross-cultural training companies, consulting companies, World Trade Center programs, and international associations that can provide valuable learning opportunities. The programs are often publicly available, but arrangements can often be made to bring them in-house for specific purposes. For instance, human resources staff can acquire training in recruiting and developing internationalist talent, administering profiling instruments to identify in-house internationalists, and career-planning systems for internationalist employees. Another program might provide tools for marketing managers responsible for planning marketing in various parts of the world; valuable internationalist education for them would include practical business implications of culturally appropriate advertising and marketing tactics for specific regions.

Peer exchanges

Just as technical professionals and managers are often sent out to help open new divisions around the world, local people working in the new divisions should come to the corporate home and visit other international locations to get the flavor of the organization worldwide. Executive and managerial interviewees from several industries mentioned peer exchanges to me—as a good idea, but not widely practiced.

These experienced internationalists saw peer exchanges as a way to facilitate cross-pollination of ideas involving everything from strategy to operations and marketing. Most of them felt that invaluable relationships could be built this way between operating units, field offices, and other levels.

Peer exchanges were seen as equally advantageous to both sides. The "home team" gets first-hand experience of internationalists from elsewhere while promoting a sense of the global organization. The visiting employees have an opportunity to meet and build relationships with those in the home offices; expatriates can keep political irons hot and lines of communication open between home and field locations. Another advantage of this intermixing was the chance to bring high-potential internationalists hired in foreign locations or divisions to the attention of the home office.

It stands to reason that such visits have to be for a genuine business purpose: a conference or a meeting of financial or marketing managers, for instance. Most people I talked with felt that it was vital they be given the opportunity to meet their peers face to face. I came to think of this as a kind of "mixmaster" internationalization process.

Culture and language training

Cross-cultural training is crucial for both the expatriate internationalist and accompanying family members, as outlined and discussed in chapter 2. Some corporations are expanding this principle to include short-term and long-term business travelers. Recall some of the observations in chapter 3, and examples from the case studies in chapter 4, about people who came into a project from the outside and expected to take charge or impose their own assumptions on a venture. This is nearly always disruptive and can harm relationships carefully built among team members. To counter that, some companies are now providing cross-cultural training programs for their international business travelers that give participants a good overview of business and social practices in the countries where they will be working.

There are several ways of accomplishing this. Cross-cultural training companies have programs designed for the business traveler. Some large corporations have sophisticated in-house training programs. Training could even be offered through a library of standardized video training modules, or through teleconference or other appropriate technology.

Some of my interviewees felt, too, that it was important to provide this kind of training at all levels within an organization— not just for those who were moving from one country to another. Internationalization is not just a one-sided issue but an every-sided issue. International businesses don't just send people out; they also bring people in. Expatriates and business travelers can come from anywhere in an organization and go anywhere else. And those who do not move around will be required at times to work with internationalists from other parts of the world, whether in person or via phone, fax, e-mail, or teleconference. Cross-cultural training provides a look into distant places and makes people aware of their own cultural imprints and how they affect business relationships in regions where the company is developing markets.

Cross-cultural work goes well beyond diversity training, which is already a part of many Western companies. While diversity training is important, it stops short of being a tool for internationalization. It primarily addresses differences in race, gender, age, ethnicity, physical ability, religion, sexual orientation, or some other clearly perceivable distinction within the national population. It does little or nothing to address fundamental cultural differences that are not obvious—the areas shown in the island model in chapter 3; and these are the factors that have proven repeatedly to be most significant in business projects around the world. Studying the history and culture that drive values is an essential basis for understanding. Beyond that, staff who deal with international employees critically need to understand their own cultural stamps before they can understand and appreciate others.

Although English is fast becoming the de facto world language—the language of business, education, science, and technology—in many parts of the world it is not widely spoken or well understood by local businesspeople or support staff. It is foolish to expect everyone in an international business situation to have equal fluency in English or any other language. Anyone leaving a country of origin for an extended time should become familiar with the basics of the host country's major language. In Europe and in some parts of Asia, it is common for educated individuals to speak at least two languages; the situation is different in the United States, a society that is notoriously unilingual.

Many tourists pick up functional language by osmosis—just soaking it up through everyday experience. This is an interesting and rather entertaining method of solving the puzzles of menus and bathrooms, but the makeshift language that results doesn't go far in business settings. And it isn't a feasible way to learn a different alphabet or other writing system.

I know, both from personal experience and from listening to many stories, that the inability to communicate is among the most alienating of experiences. My recent stint working in Ukraine is an excellent example, since my grasp of Russian is limited to the words for "ice cream" and "pencil"—not the most useful vocabulary!

Ideally, an internationalist who deliberately focuses on international studies will learn at least one second language during his or her university years. Many Western colleges and universities offering international degrees now emphasize language study, but that wasn't the case until recently. Realistically, many of the most desirable candidates for international assignments will be experienced professionals, not recent graduates; hence, many will not have been exposed to more than one language.

A basic language course is a must, and my interviewees universally and strongly pointed this out. Nothing can substitute for forms of politeness, elementary questions, and greetings. Additionally, displaying one's willingness to learn a local language goes a long way toward establishing rapport with a new group, whether in business or social settings. It is a clear demonstration of "intention" and is sincerely appreciated by host country nationals.

It's also important that accompanying spouses and family members participate in basic language study. Since they will not have the business and social interaction of an office environment, inability to communicate will isolate them, as any experienced expatriate will attest. I heard regularly about international assignments blown apart by the misery of lonely, alienated accompanying family members.

Language programs are available through many cross-cultural training companies. It's also fairly easy to find basic conversational courses through community colleges, adult education programs, Berlitz language centers, or private tutors. Once in-country, a language tutor is an important part of learning the cultural ropes and building competence for both the internationalist and the accompanying family.

Rotational assignments

Another internationalization strategy, akin to the peer exchange, is the rotational assignment, which was mentioned particularly by Asian interviewees. These short-term (three to six months) assignments are a part of the indoctrination and training of entry-level internationalists or management trainees in some large multinational companies. At mid-level, they can achieve the same purpose as the peer exchange by providing cross-pollination of ideas. An exchange employee may be a "loaned manager" with the assignment of opening a new division, providing turnaround or rescue operations, or bringing technical consulting expertise from one part of an organization to another. GTECH, a company whose Brazilian operation was profiled in chapter 4, uses this technique regularly with success. They bring managerial and technical experts from various parts of their international operations to act as advisers, experts, and internal consultants in starting up new offices.

It's important to recognize that these individuals are recruited from and sent to all parts of a worldwide organization. This "mixmaster" process was described to me as a highly effective method of making good use of internal talent while simultaneously internationalizing people at both the middle and entry levels.

Using methods like rotational assignments can present an interesting test to an in-country staff that welcomes and works with the trainees. Training and developmental programs attended by an international group of employees, or "inpatriates," can ignite cultural issues "in reverse" when a local or headquarters staff is inadequately prepared to receive them and work with them. This possibility was brought up by interviewees in Asia and North America, mainly in reference to the North Americans being unprepared either to receive an inpatriate or to be one.

The challenges faced by internationalists going out are faced equally by those coming in, and the home-based staff will need training in the cultural orientation of the newcomers. It is no longer unusual for companies to provide expatriating employees with some form of cross-cultural indoctrination. It *is* unusual, however, for companies to realize that they need the same kind of exposure for at-home employees who will be working with foreign colleagues and new recruits coming from other countries. It does little good to bring in international talent if the corporate population isn't prepared to work with them, or if they aren't prepared to become a part of the organization. In fact, companies run the risk of alienating the very people they need if they cannot manage them effectively during inpatriate or rotational assignments.

An added benefit of rotational positions and cross-cultural training opportunities is that groups from around the world mix readily and easily, blending ideas, creating sound relationships, and increasing the pool of corporate knowledge. Offshore business units and foreign offices are thus rescued from operating alone, cut off from contact with other business groups.

Project Level

Familiarization trips

Suggestions abounded during the interviews for various kinds of familiarization trips for expatriating families, ranging in length from three weeks to three months. The consensus of both Eastern and Western businesspeople was that some type of familiarization experience was crucial. The Peace Corps pre-service training process for volunteers being sent out for a two-year assignment includes a familiarization trip of up to twelve weeks, during which the volunteer lives with a host family and participates in 200 hours of language study. Only after this process is complete does the volunteer make the final commitment to accept an assignment.

While this level of immersion is probably not practical for businesses, it is an example of a program that has been thoughtfully developed with great attention to cultural implications, and it has been very successful. It is vital for both potential expatriates and their accompanying family members to have some exposure to a new environment and its culture before they are packed up and sent abroad for a period of years. They need to know what they are getting into before companies go to the very considerable expense of relocating them. (The Harvard-Amrop study calculated the international relocation expense of an executive at $300,000, exclusive of training and development.)[1]

A familiarization trip should include not just business concerns, but everyday living circumstances as well. What will it be like to find a house, go shopping, use public transportation, drive a car, deal with language problems, locate a doctor, or go to school in this new place? How can you get a phone installed, get the electricity turned on, pay bills, find a repairperson, or handle basic banking transactions? The details can be overwhelmingly complex.

Local partners and mentors

Just as corporate leaders tend to be isolated by their position, country managers, team leaders, and others outside the home environment are also isolated from the mainstream of their business. There is rarely someone to talk to, to brainstorm with, or to help with analyzing day-to-day problems. Isolation promotes anxiety, and those subjected to it begin to feel unappreciated or abandoned; this may lead them to cease trying to get help. No one person can possibly have all the answers, so an easily reachable partner is invaluable. Two kinds of "local partner" solutions were suggested during the interviews, and, interestingly, they were both suggested by Asian businesspeople.

Identifying a trusted local assistant *inside* the project environment has proven an effective tool in some cases. This individual serves as a kind of "cultural translator" for project leaders. He or she acts not as a go-between—which could become politically problematic—but as an adviser, a source of information regarding conflicts, decisions, and day-to-day activities. This aide can be a sounding board or someone to think with and to try out new ideas on. He or she can act as a checkpoint before the field management implements some policy that may prove counterproductive in a culturally unfamiliar business environment.

The drawback to employing such insiders is their possible lack of objectivity: they may fear that contradicting their superior will jeopardize their jobs. It may also be difficult in a newly formed venture to have enough history with the people in the group to know who would be an appropriate choice as cultural translator.

An alternative could be the *outsider.* Someone outside the group, but in a comparable position locally, can fill the same type of role, but with the added advantage of an objective viewpoint. This could be a local businessperson, a retired executive, someone with an interest in the venture, or someone in a local chapter of an international professional or service organization. The critical element is to have someone with whom to discuss issues and possible solutions and to brainstorm ideas, particularly as they may relate to cultural or human quandaries or public relations. Here, however, the downside could be a lack of intimate understanding of the business's internal problems or of the need for confidentiality.

In either case, finding local mentors is a valuable strategy which can greatly alleviate the sense of isolation. Here is a caution, expressed by an interviewee in Malaysia: "listening" and "heeding" are two key words. The purpose of having these mentors and cultural interpreters is to depend on their intimate understanding of the culture and business climate. It is also necessary to be willing to learn from them.

Multicultural team development

Many current and former internationalists spent a lot of time talking about the problems and challenges of pulling together a working team of multicultural members. Since it was a primary issue from their standpoint, they all had ideas about how it should (or shouldn't) be done. The following section is lengthy, but it is divided into the different phases of team development that people struggled with, and it provides ideas for each step. The specific techniques varied according to interviewees' backgrounds and those of their teams. The following suggestions for a generic team development process are a compilation of responses from consultants, cultural trainers, and internationalists who utilized a team development process to form their multicultural project groups.

A good definition of "team" appeared in a Harvard Business Review article, "The Discipline of Teams," by Jon Katzenbach and Douglas Smith, who are also authors of a book on the subject, *The Wisdom of Teams*.

> *A team is a small number of people with complementary skills who are committed to a common purpose, set of performance goals, and approach for which they hold themselves mutually accountable.*[2]

Katzenbach and Smith identify two major points: accountability and a collective work product. A team has a concrete goal to which its members are all committed. Team members take responsibility for themselves and for one another, require both individual and group accountability, and produce something concrete as a result of their individual and collective efforts. The authors go on to say that a team is more than the sum of its parts: it takes trust and a belief that each of the team members will perform in the best interests of the group goals.

Humans specialize in creating a culture whenever two or more of them form a group, an organization, or a nation. Culture dictates the rules of behavior, written or unwritten, and how human beings interact with one another. A group of robots can create a widget, but they won't create a culture.

Once established, a culture works by providing guidelines and patterns of behavior for its members. It is generational: it is passed on and can thus outlast the presence of its members. If one leaves, the culture remains. It regulates how people act and react by establishing and enforcing acceptable ways of behaving. People who step outside the norm are rebuked, and those who conform are rewarded and accepted. Simply stated, it's "how we do things here."

In universal agreement, my interviewees said:

Never underestimate the strength of culture, either organizational or national.

When people begin a business venture outside their own national and corporate comfort zone, they will assuredly deal with confusing cultural nuances of other people and other companies. As they try to make sense of this seeming chaos, they will be in a position to create a completely new cultural entity which is a blend of elements chosen from many sources. This is the "community of practice" introduced in chapter 3. By definition, this community is an instrument of group, or team, solidarity. It is an unparalleled opportunity to create this new culture with thoughtful and deliberate attention, rather than gambling that something that works will just emerge of its own accord.

Interestingly, the very efforts to respect cultural differences can sometimes gridlock a team. When professional groups assemble from various cultures, they can logically expect to encounter differences. It can happen that their polite efforts to acknowledge and respect different methods and practices lead them to defer so much that no one takes action. As international management professor Douglas Allen of the University of Denver noted, "The method of getting an intercultural team operational isn't necessarily to make everyone comfortable—but to make everyone *uncomfortable.*"[3] The trick is to recognize the best practices regardless of where they come from, and to adopt them as ideals of team behavior. This will inevitably cause discomfort in some circles, but discomfort drives change. And change is what moves groups forward, forcing them to try new ways of working together and altering their individual and collective behavior to create a culture unique to their own new community.

Figure 6 displays a cluster of team objectives. With five major points and one anchoring element, the objectives logically organize in the shape of a star. Metaphorically, the symbol of the

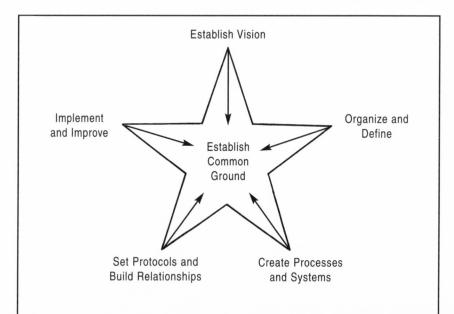

Figure 6. Pre-Team, Select the Right Leader. *The Star Team process. At each point, the team returns again to the anchor, the common ground. If conflict occurs, no matter what point the team has reached, return again to the anchor. Without the anchor, the team ceases to be a community.*

star is appropriate for the images that it evokes: a positive force, shining, a part of something larger, celestial. Each point of the star represents one objective of team development. These can cross-link with one another as the team works continually to check and reinforce its processes and progress, returning regularly to the anchor.

Only when teams unite can they effectively take on the responsibility of an entire work segment or project, make day-to-day decisions about how it is to be accomplished, solve problems, manage customer service, maintain quality standards, and share leadership roles. By granting the team collective authority to make decisions about how their work is to be accomplished, the individual team members become increasingly effective, realize job satisfaction, achieve a high level of productivity, and develop a sense of responsibility and pride.

The premise

The first step in team-building is to accept that tossing a team together and expecting it to work efficiently is short-sighted. The second is to heed the experience of the seasoned internationalists and interculturalists who have told their stories. All the strategic plans and financing schemes in the world will come undone if a group of people are trying to implement them in a hostile, change-resistant, or apathetic work environment. The third step is to utilize a team development process that—given the right combination of strategy, people, and motivation—can bring about exceptional business results.

Team leadership

Before a team can form, it must have a leader. Selecting leaders for multicultural teams poses an interesting challenge. This is the ideal place for the internationalist. However, as we have seen, the traditional Western approach of recruiting people who have the right mix of technical skills frequently fails to consider the internationalist mindset—the characteristics identified in chapter 2. These are flexibility, curiosity, a willingness to set aside preconceived notions about how things ought to be done, and an open mind.

The Internationalists

At a round-table for international managers, one very experi-enced internationalist summarized a list of critical characteristics which he felt represented the ideal mix for success as an interna-tionalist team leader:

- Flexibility and passion for new experiences
- Global mindset
- Intellectual curiosity
- Attitude of compromise
- Ability to deal with constantly changing situations
- High tolerance for ambiguity
- Motivation

Some executives I interviewed testified that it's hard to find people who are both technically and culturally adept and who will accept an assignment that moves them (and their families) abroad or interrupts their chosen career path:

> *I would say that in our company the first thing we look for is willingness. Being an internationalist was not one of the requisites for being hired. We have enough people who can't leave here ... we need people who actually want to go overseas.*
>
> Director of Asia Pacific division of a worldwide manufacturer

If ideal candidates are hard to come by, and the only real candidate is the willing one, the assigning authority should quickly realize that there are some pieces missing. The Overseas Assignment Inventory (OAI) instrument discussed in chapter 2 can be an effective means of mitigating the problems of blending technical criteria with characteristics for team leadership positions. The instrument analyzes candidates' responses in the following critical areas: expectations, openmindedness, respect for beliefs, trust, discomfort tolerance, personal control, flexi-bility, patience, social adaptability, initiative, risk-taking, sense of humor, interpersonal interest, and spousal communication. It then measures the responses against a norm that denotes success levels in each area. With these measurements in hand, it is possible to assess a potential team leader's areas of strength and weakness and direct professional coaching to help develop him or her for an assignment. It's a sensible assumption that people who want to work in a foreign locale will also want to be successful at it. If they are aware of potential stress points in advance, they will be much better prepared to deal with them when they arise.

Multicultural team leadership is a lot of work. Team leaders report that they spend as much time managing the relationships among their team members as they do on the actual business of the business. They are constantly balancing and rebalancing emphases between the tasks and the human issues of motivation, clarification of goals, and focus on team performance.

In joint ventures, strategic alliances, or other cooperative ventures between companies, team members will be coming from different organizational, technical, and cultural backgrounds. One interviewee commented on the difficulties of getting the management team going: "Jockeying for political position with their constituencies became a regular event, with the focus more on themselves as individuals than on the group." Even when a company assigns an expatriate to a wholly owned foreign subsidiary, that person will be dealing with organizational and social situations that demand new ways of thinking and acting.

Stephen Rhinesmith[4] has identified three major areas that leaders must deal with when developing an effective multicultural work group. They are planning, organizing, and leading. Each of these areas is significantly influenced by culturally determined factors. Leaders need to learn where the basic differences are and anticipate where problems may arise as a result of cultural variations in behavior. The internationalist characteristics are a critical element in their ability to do this.

The anchor: Establish common ground

Once the all-important leader is selected and in place, the next stage is anchoring the group to what they have in common. This anchor provides the center to which all the points are tied and the

156 · The Internationalists

foundation to which the group will return again and again during
the life of the project. Building the team begins here.

After a group has been assembled, the task of pulling it
together begins with identifying what its individual members have
in common. Multicultural groups often come from backgrounds
that are radically different—always culturally, and frequently organizationally as well. It's a challenge in the beginning to see one
another as anything but dissimilar. Before they can begin to
function at all, they need to find some anchoring commonalities.

Establishing the anchor depends on the ability of the team
members to identify with one another somehow beyond the fact
that they are all in the same room with a somewhat similar notion
of what they're doing there. Mediation technique often begins with
the mediator searching for something the parties share. It can be
small things: for instance, that they are all about the same age, or
they all have college degrees, or they have similar technical or
functional backgrounds. The idea is for the members to come up
with a list of commonalities. When difficulties arise, team leaders
can help correct the course by returning to what they have in
common, rather than focusing on what is dividing them.

A simple, elegant and very practical suggestion came from a
consultant who witnessed a creative and powerfully unifying
process in Taiwan. The president of a multinational joint venture
company had the members of the management team read selected
books and then meet in informal groups to discuss the content and
ideas. He chose the books carefully to anchor a business practice he
wanted the group to think about. Some of the choices were *Built To
Last, Delivering on the Promise,* and *Customer Satisfaction Is
Worthless, Customer Loyalty Is Priceless.*

Each month at the leadership meeting of all supervisors in the
company, the team of about forty broke into small, preassigned
groups to discuss segments informally, taking perhaps one or two
chapters of the current book. No one was forced to speak. They
shared ideas; they talked about their perceptions of the book, how
they thought it could be applied to their work, the relevance in their
own country, conflicts with their culture, and their own experiences; they shared suggestions, assessments, and learnings from the

book. The practice provided an enormously fertile opportunity to explore and understand differences and to create ways in which the group could work together. It was culture-building at its core.

This process is completely unstructured (with the exception of cautioning the American participants not to "take charge"), and it has proven to be a brilliant way of cementing learning from the selected readings, using a common language, and providing a common frame of reference when an issue or problem arises that needs to be worked out. The process of using book discussions to discover commonalities can work equally well to help the group establish and keep a common vision—the next step in the team-building process.

Establish common vision

This point was mentioned in chapter 1 as one of the most universal and difficult of problems in international enterprises. Time and again, my interviewees from all four continents brought it up as a critical hindsight issue.

Once the team members have established their anchor point of personal, professional, or organizational commonalities, they will recognize that they have ways to identify with one another. Then they can begin to formulate a common vision. It's easy to think that a multicultural team assembled for a joint venture would naturally have the same purpose in mind. However, this is rarely true. They may know in general what their respective leaders have said their goal is, but because the members come from various cultural and organizational backgrounds, they also think and plan and organize differently. They come into the venture with different values, ways of working, and understandings.

Titan Wang of AC Nielson Taiwan commented:

> *[It's difficult] particularly for those companies who are all successful, they have their own reputations in the market. They just don't think that the other company deserves to work with them under the same roof or in the same office. [You should make sure] that you have one company in the office, not more.*[5]

Team members frequently have very different personal agendas as well. Recall the earlier comment by Malaysian executive Chow Chee Yan: "Just because you share the same bed, doesn't mean you have the same dream." These are powerful testaments to the need to create that special "third culture," a community which is a blend of its disparate parts.

Team leaders need to pull out all their internationalist skills to get to this vital stage. Common purpose is challenging to establish when group members have culturally ingrained behaviors that dictate whether it's appropriate to speak up, offer an opinion, challenge, or disagree. Yet without this interaction, the group is likely to wind up at cross-purposes, paying more attention to individual constituencies than to the project goals. If they have differing ideas of what their purpose is, they will be hard pressed to identify what methods they are going to employ to achieve it.

Unless team leaders establish a common vision early on, the team will not unite, and members will focus continually on what keeps them apart—the "us versus them" syndrome. Thus, defining vision is the essence of team-building, providing clarity of purpose and identifying the road the group will travel together. With a common vision, the team can see what makes them unique, and that essential "third culture" can develop.

Differences will arise regarding basic values, market understanding, organizational purposes and goals, and personal culture-bound beliefs. Often the envisioning process involves making implicit knowledge explicit; the leader's sensitivity and analytic skills take the lead in this. Most important, however, is the establishment of a purpose that goes beyond the individual members and becomes a goal of the team itself. It should be explicit and should include *what* they are going to do, *for whom* they will do it, and *why,* or the result they are seeking. The result should be defined in a way that articulates its value for each member as well as for the group.

During this process, specific performance goals will emerge that become subsets of the total vision. Goals identify what the team itself will do. At the end, each team member can articulate the purpose of the team as a unit, and its goals, in language that is understood by all members. Commitment and a sense of responsibility to the goals that all helped to define can result from this unifying process.

Organize and define

Next, the group can determine how they will organize themselves and define the roles and processes they will need to accomplish their goals. In this phase, the roles of the various team members should be clearly stated and decisions made about how they will operate in a complementary fashion. Team members can now begin to organize into a series of subteams, or committees, which fulfill different important functions: budget, administration, training, recognition and rewards, and so on.

As this phase unfolds, expect a storm of cultural issues. Culture deeply influences how the team members see themselves in relation to the others. The operative differences may be rooted in national culture, in corporate culture, and even in the communities of practice represented by different professional disciplines. In Rhinesmith's analysis of this segment of team development, he talks about authority, roles, control, staff and line relationships, job descriptions, formal or informal relationships, committees, and flexibility: all are culturally influenced.

Authority structures within the team will be influenced by cultural perceptions of the importance of the individual and the ways status is determined. Roles or job descriptions will be affected by motivation, flexibility, and commitment to action. Intergroup relationships will respond to social alliances, relationships between genders or age groups, individual versus group orientation, and communication styles. Team and subteam meetings will be affected by authority issues, and by willingness to express opinions.

As intimidating as all these issues may seem, pattern differences need not cause total immobility. A good team development process is fairly generic, whether applied within a single culture or in a multitude of cultures represented in one group. However, recognizing where these differences arise and being able to identify what is behind organizational and role challenges can go a long way toward bringing about agreement in a multicultural group.

Create processes and systems

Teams can't function without the right tools and infrastructure. Technology and systems should be identified early on so the group will have the appropriate hardware and software support, telephony, and administrative help. Here corporate leadership support is important, since these needs should be included in the budget for the team.

As a sidelight to the discussion of systems, a few people brought up the fact that teams now are often challenged by not working in the same place. With the increasing use of e-mail, private-access web sites, and specialized software, virtual teams are materializing, which creates a whole new category of issues. It's not impossible to build an effective team from distant parts; however, the prevailing view of internationalists and executives seemed to be that even if teams met often in a virtual environment, face-to-face meetings were also critical, particularly in the early formative process and relationship-building period.

Tasks and timing are also a part of system creation. Cultural differences can significantly influence how this process plays out. In determining how tasks will be carried out, thinking patterns emerge that will affect the level of risk-taking, the use of scientific methodology, the amount of information needed for decision-making, problem-solving methods, flexibility, and even the nature of the task itself.

The group should also begin to establish a common vocabulary by identifying terms and phrases—professional and technical jargon—that they regularly use in their work. These may have to be defined and explained so that they all understand one another's communications. The Becton-Dickinson case study in chapter 4 provides a good example of the significance of defining common terms.

The cultural dimension of time perception was discussed in chapter 3, and it's easy to guess how this issue will arise. Anglo and Northern European linear thinkers with perceptions organized around steps, sequence, and linear accomplishment of goals will adjust easily to established timing and indeed may insist on it. In contrast, the spiral-time adherents will not so easily adapt to dictated, rigid timelines. A skilled internationalist can lead the team to a compromise solution and manage the inevitable upheavals along the way.

Set protocols and build relationships

Establishing team customs and finding out what the other guy is like helps to align the group on their common path. Here are some initial questions:

- What are the team members' work styles?
- How do the members relate to the leader?
- How do they relate to one another?
- What are their various ways of expressing thoughts and ideas?
- What are their various ways of treating deadlines?
- What are the values of these different ways. and how can they best be used to achieve the goal?
- What are some places where difficulties may arise, and how can these be addressed within the group?

Cultural nuances often shade the meanings of work relationships. The questions above can serve as a guide for leaders to unearth some of these differences in methods, bring them to the group consciousness, and open them for recognition. Once differences are discovered and acknowledged, protocols can be worked out that can establish a working methodology for the group. This isn't an easy step, however. People everywhere have a tendency to resist or even sabotage change and new ways of doing things. This is not surprising if it is understood that change is driven by discomfort.

As team members begin to understand and acknowledge differences, they will begin to uncover ways in which they will have to adjust their own styles, changing and redefining their own uniqueness in terms of their team experience. Then they can create and revise as needed the essential methods that allow the team to operate. As they begin to identify their different ways of working and thinking, they can build agreements on processes and establish effective relationships with each other, understanding the value that each one contributes.

Implement and improve

Putting the whole process into action brings reality to the goals. They become concrete rather than theoretical. Adding a sense of urgency starts the project moving and keeps it going. Plugging in a continuous improvement plan can help the group define what more they need in the way of advice, tools, support, or technology. Making a commitment to continuous improvement also allows for flexibility of planning and revision of timing—an important component when dealing with differences in time perception. Internationalist leaders will deal with the issue of flexibility in role redefinition and cultural awareness as they work to initiate continuous improvement plans.

To do this, a group needs a feedback strategy. Team members can use a self-established method to find out how they are perceived by the others and how they can work more effectively together. Feedback, of course, goes both ways. Perhaps a good question for team members to ask each other is "How are *we* doing?"—instead of asking about "me" or "you." This keeps the focus on the group rather than the individual, yet allows space for constructive comments. How this process is built will depend on the makeup of the team and the cultures from which they come. It could be a one-on-one process, a group process, or a leader-facilitated process. Alternatively, a third-party team-builder might come in at regular intervals to facilitate, see where the team is, and help keep them together. This can forestall a tendency to slip back into an "us versus them" situation by giving members regular opportunities to course-correct during the life of a project.

Understandably, not all team members will respond to feedback in the same way. How and where feedback occurs should be carefully considered, keeping in mind the cultural issues surrounding relationship with authority, outspokenness, face-saving, and methods of dealing with conflict. This is a place to take great care not to sabotage team effectiveness with unthinking, blunt, "in-your-face" constructive criticism. Positive feedback should accompany any meeting of this type. People everywhere respond to private praise, and it can go a long way toward softening a difficult feedback encounter.

Rewards, recognition and celebration are all important; and again, the makeup of the team and the project budget will determine what kind of reward mechanism will be most effective and how it is best delivered. Common reward systems include additional pay for skills acquired or skills used, bonus awards for reaching group or individual performance goals, or nonmonetary awards such as group activities, trophies, or certificates of recognition. The team should decide together how they would like to celebrate their successes.

Closing the loop

Many people mentioned their frustration in dealing with a home-office corporate leadership who did not really understand the depth and breadth of circumstances in the field. This caused premature withdrawal from projects, wasting of resources, lost revenues, scapegoating, or early return of expatriates. A frequent object of complaint was the unrealistic demands of managers whose view of the business venture was limited to financial spreadsheets.

Internationalists who lead projects in other countries need the support of those at the top, but they also have a responsibility to make sure that they are accurately and completely aware of what's going on at home. Like most other human endeavors, it's a two-way street. Some internationalist interviewees recommended practical executive education tours and trips so that corporate leaders could see at first hand what was happening in the field. This definitely closes the loop. During these trips, with a captive audience, project leaders can describe in detail their challenges, successes, plans, and ideas. They can also present their cases for what needs to change and why, with demonstrations at hand to prove their points. The executive gets to have a real-time internationalization experience, and the internationalist keeps in touch with leadership—something many returned expatriates felt had been missing from their personal experiences.

Other strategies included regular and detailed reporting back through channels, with elements such as culture briefings, photographs, and slide presentations. Expatriates made it a point to visit the corporate home periodically to present these reports. This is not only an effective strategy for keeping leaders informed of the real story about international projects, it has the added advantage of being a superb career management tool. It can help to prevent the "out of sight, out of mind" syndrome lamented by many returned expatriates. The key is a commitment to closing this loop, no matter which method or combination of methods is used.

Summary

International business deals are proliferating at such a rate that projects are being created regularly, and their members represent more and more diversity. Tactics that can be employed to increase success rates include:

- practical executive education and experiences
- volunteer projects
- continuing education
- peer exchanges
- culture and language training
- rotational assignments
- familiarization trips
- local partners and mentors
- multicultural team development

A team development process, uniting people from different organizational and national backgrounds, is a vital factor in achieving business success.

Business goals decided on between venture partners have to be implemented and nurtured toward success. This won't happen without cultural clashes between differing corporate styles, national cultures, and even functional areas. Internationalists play a vital role in achieving corporate goals, using leadership skills that include the ability to regularly deal with ambiguity and to suspend judgement about rightness and wrongness. Team leadership is a real talent; multicultural team leadership raises it to another level and requires both business expertise and a finely tuned intuitive sense about human interaction.

In the final analysis, it isn't one brilliant moment that creates a successful international business venture, but an organization-wide, consistent line of common thought and common practices applied again and again.

6

Worldwide Partners
An Organization of Internationalists

During the conceptual stage of writing this book, I was inspired by a woman I met, Patricia Fiske, and the organization she leads—Worldwide Partners. There was something different about the way they worked in the world—something that appealed to me on an instinctual level. I was hard pressed at the time to explain that appeal, but as I began my travels and interviews, I came to recognize and define what was unique about them: they have applied the characteristics and definition of the internationalist at an organizational level.

Fiske personifies the internationalist, and Worldwide Partners is full of them. They combine exceptional industry knowledge and technical skills with personal characteristics that make them a global force. They have built a fascinating culture that is bigger and better than the sum of its parts.

Worldwide Partners is not a traditional company in the structural sense, but rather a network of independently owned companies that have knit themselves closely together to become much more than a loose association. They share a guiding philosophy, inspired leadership, a clear mission, and a work-force that believes wholeheartedly in all these elements.

This organization operates in a fashion that reverses the traditional corporate model. The headquarters is small and acts as a communication center though which information flows as it responds to the requests and needs of the worldwide offices. As president, Fiske assumes the role of a steward-leader, moving around the world to attend meetings and to facilitate individual and regional strengthening. The regional and local groups clearly and definitely make their own organizing and operating decisions, in direct contrast to most Western-style organizations, in which headquarters makes policy, establishes practices, and directs traffic.

I chose to set down their story because their uniqueness appealed to my Western-educated brain. They are organic, they are chaotic, they are constantly *becoming*. They grow, contract, create, change, rework, talk, argue, and then do it again. In short, they evolve.

What they have, and what I recognized instinctively, is something I would call "congruence." There is a prevailing sense of common purpose, of commitment and trust that comes from everywhere in the company. They all replied similarly when asked to describe their organization, and yet none of them seemed rootbound. That is, they did not identify as an "American" or "French" or "Indonesian" company. They quite simply belonged to the world.

Here is their story, developed from first-person interviews and from regional focus groups I conducted with people from all parts of the far-flung organization.

• • •

"You can't e-mail trust," says Worldwide Partners president Patricia Fiske from the network headquarters in Denver, Colorado. A concise style and business philosophy are reflected in this new-century organization—a partnership in spirit, not contract. Internationally, Worldwide Partners numbers 90 independent marketing communications companies located in 40 countries. With billings of $3.7 billion per year, they employ more than 5,000 professionals representing more than 2,000 clients, living and breathing cultural differences with cross-border advertising campaigns.

The bonding agent in Worldwide Partners is trust. They operate with a philosophy and practice based on keeping commitments, trusting each other, and working collaboratively. Cutting-edge technology enables the network to function successfully as a business yet remain emphatically human. Trust enables the people of five continents to work together in fluid, flexible teams, coming together for sales and client service, disbanding and reforming for the next collaboration.

A testament to vision and values, the multicultural network exists and prospers in a world of intense competition, corporate secrecy and distrust, intelligence snooping, and international wheeling and dealing. They have successfully created a global business force, yet they have maintained individual identities and integrity.

To sustain and enhance their enviable human quality, the far-flung staff members regularly meet face to face for regional conferences, and annually as a worldwide network. At those times, building relationships, honoring one another, sharing ideas and knowledge, and thinking of new ways to work together brings them closer as Worldwide Partners.

At the organization's 1997 World Conference in Buenos Aires, the trust and friendship among the principals was apparent. The Argentine partner's pride was clear as he welcomed colleagues to his city. Throughout the four days of meetings, the group worked together, shared their best practices and ideas, experimented with new methods of client service using virtual technology, and celebrated successes.

At the regional meetings that took place during the four-day world conference, I asked the partners to describe Worldwide Partners as an organization. Without exception, the groups used the word "trust." Other concepts they offered were friendship, collaboration, partners, experienced, multicultural, and fun. Clearly, the vision is shared among the partners throughout the world.

Who They Are

Founded in 1938 as the American Advertising Agency Network (AAAN) with five original members, Worldwide Partners began as an advertising agency network conceived as a way for small agencies to help one another. Renamed 3AI in 1988, it continued to grow as a network until 1996, when it was renamed Worldwide Partners and began its evolution into a "brand." The emergence of the network as a business entity is a natural development in the advertising industry, where loose networks have never been unusual. Worldwide Partners, however, has gone a step farther by organizing into more formal regional groups representing Asia-Pacific, Europe, Latin America, and North America. They look to the headquarters in Denver to provide a unifying influence.

Describing themselves as "multilocal" instead of "multinational," the partners team collaboratively, acting as branch offices for one another in offering sales and client service around the world. The headquarters uses the latest in web technology to maintain a private access web site where partners can meet in real time. International accounts can be serviced from anywhere in the world through a web site that provides instant access to the latest account information for partners across 24 time zones. Their cooperative efforts serve clients' local needs as well as client companies' expansion into new markets. In the words of one partner:

> We're fast and we're smart. In our culture we have no management structure and thus no organizational layers. Everyone is on the front line and has a real sense of ownership.

A worldwide network made up of independent advertising agencies of different sizes, from widely divergent cultural backgrounds, representing very different clients, sounds like a recipe for organizational chaos. In fact, diversity is the network's strongest asset. Working together, the multicultural partners bring a major advantage to client service. They are able to address sensitive cultural issues that, if ignored, could spell failure for a new product in an unfamiliar country. Local presence, local relationships, and intimate understanding of cultural nuances can bring great benefit, for example, to a Canadian company expanding into Southeast Asia. Of equal value is the ability of the independent partners to market to an existing multinational corporation, as either a regional or global entity, ensuring service and attention in local markets.

The Dyneon account is a notable example of the collaborative efforts of Worldwide Partners to secure major international business. Dyneon, LLC, a joint venture involving the fluoropolymer business of 3M and Hoechst, awarded the marketing communications contract to Worldwide Partners after a long, consultant-supported search because, they said, "as an entrepreneurial enterprise, we wanted a partner with passion, excitement and zest."

The fact that each partner agency is indigenously owner-managed was the key for Dyneon. The market-to-market knowledge promised solutions that were truly culturally appropriate. Worldwide Partners has a rule of principal-to-principal communication that avoids long hierarchical structures and allows quick decisions. Commitments are high because the partner agencies have a stake in the client's success. Dyneon likes Worldwide Partners' proactivity and the integrated global marketing communication recommendations.

The campaign for Dyneon was created in a joint retreat meeting in Munich, Germany, with participation of the U.S. lead agency in Chicago and input from agencies in all the Dyneon markets. Personal meetings, video and telephone conferences, and the Dyneon Intranet—which was created by Worldwide Partners— enable close cooperation among the agencies in various world regions and their numerous partners within the international client organization.

How They Do It

A significant reason why Worldwide Partners works well is that the partners have learned how to compensate one another for advice and service. There are no set fees. Arrangements are made between the partners at the time assistance is provided. Payment for internal services effectively produces a quid pro quo situation, eliminating the problem of one partner not responding to requests for assistance from another.

Competition and "turf" issues that are problems for many centrally owned and managed companies are often avoided because most of these partners do not compete with one another for business. Neither do they vie to achieve corporately established profit margins and sales goals, or to get internal jobs and promotions.

Selection

Finding potential partners to join this worldwide team is a challenge. It is Fiske's task to expand the network, which has tripled in size since she took the helm in 1987. She says she selects new partners in two distinct ways: by business analysis and by human instinct.

For an advertising and marketing communications network, a decision for growth is based on identifying a geographic market with an economy that supports the expansion of products and services to the public. Once this is identified, partners are consulted for recommendations and local advertising associations are contacted for referrals. That is followed by rigorous interviews of potential members to assess quality of work, financial capabilities, and community reputation. Client lists are examined. Finally, when all due diligence is complete, Fiske and the regional partners apply the final test: Do the prospective partners think in global and local terms simultaneously? Is the chemistry right? Will the candidate keep commitments and uphold the trust of other partners? Are they flexible and creative? In other words, do they act organizationally like internationalists? If these hurdles are crossed, the potential partner is presented to the whole company on a ballot for their vote.

Teams within teams

Headquarters

"It's chaos," says a member of the headquarters team. "The organization is alive. We're in a constant state of change." This versatile team has been called "the Great Knitters" for their ability to hold it all together. When I asked them to brainstorm the key elements of the headquarters group, the concepts that emerged were trust, local focus, vision, leadership, and integrity—words that mirrored the responses of the partners around the world.

They emphasized that technology is only a vehicle to foster human connections, but they all agree that the absolute key to success is fast, dependable communications. "We answer the phone as though we expect to find our best friend on the other end," says one key staff member.

Headquarters supports itself through fees for services and other financing arrangements engineered by region and circumstance. Acting as a facilitator, the headquarters team serves as a communications and information clearinghouse for the partners. An extensive database of current client experience worldwide is centrally maintained so that it is accessible to all partners. Any agency can send a request and receive an answer and assistance within 24 hours. Communications technology is constantly being updated and improved, overseen by an in-house webmaster and all-around technowizard. Other services provided by the headquarters team are talent resources, media management services, syndicated research products, on-line research services, a consultant database, and a library. Legal and financial training and consulting services are available on request. The team also plans and coordinates all world and regional meetings.

In addition to the client-service advantages of the private access web site, committees can conduct virtual meetings through real-time internal chat groups. This venue also carries weekly publications, newsletters, and other communications from headquarters.

Committees

Fluid teams form and disband as committees to address opportunities and issues. Standing committees are chaired by partners on a rotating basis and operated by the board of directors.

One of the more interesting committees is the Vitality Plan, which supports several subcommittees beneath it. Acting as a feeder tank of new ideas, it is constantly replenished by members representing the various regions. The committee sets priorities and liaises with action forces to implement plans, and it cross-links with finance because, as the controller succinctly puts it, "Some miracles are not in the budget."

Action forces are committees formed to address specific issues. They are chaired by a "champion" or advocate, and they disband when the issue is resolved.

Regional teams

Regionally, four world groups face individual sets of inter-cultural and organizational challenges. Ethnic populations or cultural norms and behaviors differ within regions and even within countries. Regional partners are encouraged to be creative in how they work together. They decide among themselves how they will be structured and make collective decisions about how to collaborate.

Business opportunities are escalating in Latin America. In this world region, individual relationships are extremely important to business success, and the ability of one partner to introduce regional comrades personally to a major client is a distinct advantage. Advertising needs to be culturally fine-tuned, because cross-border issues exist within the region. Worldwide Partners' agencies in Latin America have begun to organize and operate a regional holding company. They have been successful in acquiring major clients by positioning themselves as a regional network with global partners rather than as independent local agencies or as a multinational organization.

In the Asia-Pacific region, the partners began to operate five years ago as a joint business team to market services to multinational and growing clients. Because each agency's focus is in a different country, it has the advantages of individual market knowledge and contacts, an understanding of cultural nuances within the Asia-Pacific region, and the capability to assist clients across regional borders. The network has become a powerful multi-local force in this part of the world, with flexibility and local presence in almost every country.

The European group operates differently. Its members are spread throughout the United Kingdom, Western Europe, and Scandinavia, and it is becoming a presence in the emerging markets of Eastern Europe. A few of the powerful Western European agencies collaborated to form a European Joint Business Team, a cooperative entity intended to sell and to serve clients by presenting a united front. The Joint Business Team has spread through the entire European region, with marketing and support materials to promote joint efforts.

The Scandinavian countries have traditionally been recognized as a unit with many common interests, and as a result the five partners there frequently work together. With a less formal structure than the holding company concept of the Latin American group, this group nevertheless represents a significant presence in cross-border marketing communications in the dynamic economies of Western Europe.

Shared business in the European region has produced an interesting result. An important client of the German partner is YTONG, a manufacturer of building blocks for the construction industry, which began buying plants in Eastern Europe. To ensure continued client service, the German partner, along with president Fiske, actively recruited small agencies in the emerging markets of Poland and Hungary. These new partner agencies immediately repositioned the advertising devised for the German market into appropriate campaigns for their particular markets. Mentored by the German agency, the energetic new partners quickly established themselves as successful independent agencies in their own right.

North America, the largest of the regions, is divided into three districts—Eastern, Central, and Western. It is here that the company finds the biggest challenge in achieving a collaborative team spirit. In the United States and Canada, competition and independence have traditionally characterized both business and individual behavior. However, a shift toward a more collaborative business model is occurring. Some of the North American partner agencies have had notable success with joint marketing. They have teamed to make successful presentations to large national and international businesses with interests in the United States and Canada as well as around the world.

The Alaska Seafood Marketing Institute selected the Anchorage-based partner agency for account service and media placement in targeted markets. The Alaskan agency teamed with the Chicago partner agency to give the client just what it wanted: a local touch with a national reach. "The key to winning the account," said the Alaskan Worldwide Partners agency head, "was the two agencies working cooperatively."

To balance traditional American competitive habits, seventeen of the fifty-one North American partner agencies met in February 1997 in Dallas to participate in a process called "Relationships Built on Trust" or RBT. During the daylong showcase meeting, billed as an internal trade show, each attending partner made a presentation of its most prominent capabilities. Areas of expertise and best practices were offered as resources to other partners to broaden and enhance the capabilities of all.

Client service teams

A major client of the Buenos Aires agency was introduced at the 1997 World Conference. The advertising challenge he presented was to introduce a traditional, indigenous South American product, the herbal tea beverage yerba maté, to the world market. In an experimental working model using only computers linked together via the Internet, the world group divided into regions and districts, each meeting in a different room, and communicated only on line. Within twenty-four hours they devised a global positioning strategy and presented culturally appropriate, total marketing communications campaigns to introduce the product in their separate regions.

This exercise was introduced at the conference as a challenge to use technology in new ways and to allow the partners to become something more than they had ever attempted. The result was remarkable. The client was delighted, and the partners had a stimulating new experience in using virtual technology.

Mentorship

In keeping with the trust and team spirit of the entire network, European regional agencies, as well as the entire Worldwide Partners group, have served as mentors to the fledgling agencies in Hungary and Poland. The mentorship trend promises to continue as the network expands.

Mentorship is an unstructured process in the network. It can take the form of education, information, or financial breaks. Because the bedrock of the organization is trust, any agency in need of information or assistance can call on the headquarters team to put them in touch with a partner who is an expert in their area of need. The call for assistance is answered within twenty-four hours, and a plan is put in motion. In addition, small developing agencies are frequently given financial breaks when they access the services of the headquarters or other partners. The philosophy of the universal win prevails: when one agency wins business and prospers, it enhances the interest of all.

Challenges

Headquarters team admits that the network has its problems. Shared vision matters. Interestingly, it is in the United States that the cultural norms of competition and individualism pose the most direct test to this vision. Some U.S. partners are slower to subscribe to the new ideas of a powerful, globally networked force, although the more progressive agencies in this region have been quick to position themselves as global players.

The themes of change, chaos, flexibility, and rapid market and business shifts continually emerge. None of the partners can predict conditions much beyond the next year. The speed of globalization affects this business radically, necessitating continuing movement toward cooperation, collaboration, and trust. Because the partners are increasingly pulled (and sometimes pushed) together, their ability to transcend the issues of culture takes on increasing importance.

Language barriers challenge communications around the world. When information is shared from the Denver headquarters, it goes out in English, the common language of the network. Meetings are also conducted in English. But English is not the native language of half the partners. Communicating news and information can be an interesting task. English idioms and other expressions are not always understood by those whose native language is Thai, Spanish, or Hungarian. A multilingual headquarters staffer helps solve some of these issues, but it remains a demanding—if sometimes humorous—task.

The Future

Worldwide Partners believes that certain attitudes are absolutely critical to their success as a true partnership. The partners are recognized for success in their individual markets. As a regional and global force, they must continue to strive for the shift in attitude that positions them as global players, among themselves as well as to potential clients. They frequently ask each other the question, "What could we be if we let ourselves?"

What makes Worldwide Partners extraordinary is the bond of trust that allows them to meet challenges with inspired leadership, commitment, communication, technology, flexibility, and superior people. Fiske admits that she views the organization through rose-colored glasses. She says that her job is "to understand the dreams of our partners and to bring the resources of the partners worldwide to make those dreams come true."

In the advertising business, the agency that ignores the cultural differences inherent in its clients' cross-border marketing efforts will fail. Worldwide Partners doesn't just bring sensitive intercultural knowledge to its client companies; the partners also practice it among themselves. The ability of this network to share candidly, to respect and accept individual and cultural differences, and to support a world vision about how they work together, is a model for other international organizations. The creative use of multicultural teams, coupled with the latest in communications technology, enables Worldwide Partners to be flexible and fluid, changing and evolving with the demands of business.

7

Conclusion:
On Becoming an Internationalist

*It is far better to have seen it once than to have heard of
it one thousand times.*

—Mongolian proverb

The message of this book is that the internationalist is an individual, not a company. That individual is unique, possessing
specific personal characteristics as well as specific competencies in
a particular field. Recognizing the internationalists and placing
value on their capabilities will have a profound effect on corporate
mind-set and on the ways global companies organize themselves in
relationship to their important human capital.

Near the end of my research and writing, I was asked by the
director of a graduate program in international management if I
thought it was possible to become an internationalist by studying in
an international degree program. I paused: not because I didn't
have an answer, but because I was loath to state straightforwardly
what I instinctively wanted to say. Now, however, I stand by my
original impulse. The answer, I believe, is no. It's not something

that can be taught. But before you decide to throw something in my general direction, let me continue by saying that I sincerely believe that it can be *learned*. There is a difference.

Just as my personal experience in the world caused me to reach inside myself and bring out characteristics I didn't know I had, so it is with others who have become internationalists, as I did, by default. How much easier it would be if internationalists were recognized, recruited, supported, and developed by corporations to start with! In becoming members of a recognized and identified profession, internationalists assume a completely different role in their organizations and in the world. It becomes a professional field for which people *can* prepare.

The internationalist is a missing link in international business. We often do not have the right people in the right jobs because we have not properly identified the requirements for working in foreign locales. Certainly most of the technical requirements and skills have been analyzed and identified. But that, as we have seen, is not the whole story. Companies and their projects have frequently failed because individuals selected to work overseas did not possess the necessary internationalist characteristics. Business experience and technical knowledge are not enough. Willingness to live overseas is not enough. They must possess the right mix of experience, technical knowledge, characteristics, and attitudes.

If becoming an internationalist is not something that can be taught, then how *do* people learn to be internationalists? They learn it by doing it. And that, in a nutshell, is why I believe that curiosity is the most important of the characteristics of the internationalist. People who are not curious will not care to learn.

Corporations can establish "internationalizing" programs that will go a long way toward creating an internal pool of internationalist talent. Graduate schools can provide international learning, internships, and volunteer experiences that offer wide exposure. Students can begin to think of their careers in a new way. Instead of just making a decision to obtain a degree in international management, they can acquire both the degree and field experiences that will test the characteristics and attitudes they must develop. Then they can begin to see themselves as "professional internationalists."

In closing, I offer a short list of maxims culled from my interviews, my analyses, and informal conversations in the course of my travels. They sum up the findings and offer the key to this book's goal.

Corporations need to broaden the concept of who is of value to the organization.

Internationalists are individuals with specific talents and characteristics who can be identified and recruited. They represent a new profession for a new century.

Companies that wish to be global must learn to find and keep internationalists and use them as the glue to keep cross-border ventures aligned with corporate goals.

Companies can use internationalists to globalize their strategies and systems from inside, using specific tools and processes.

Companies themselves then begin to reflect the characteristics of the internationalist.

My wish for the reader is to acknowledge what I have come to firmly believe: that the internationalist truly is a new profession for a new century. Embrace it.

Afterword

No one writes a book in a vacuum, although it sometimes feels like it. The experiences of the past year and a half profoundly affected my view of the world and its businesspeople. To those who participated in the formal interview process, my deepest thanks. For those who made connections for me, my gratitude is yours. And for those who encouraged and assisted me in countless other ways, I could not have done it without you.

In the interest of continuing the research I began (and I expect it will never be concluded), I would like to invite anyone who reads this book to share an internationalist experience or a story. Please write to me or send me e-mail. I correspond regularly with people in all parts of the world, and I welcome your tales. Tell me your experiences, your problems, and your solutions.

I plan to write another book about internationalists. At this point I cannot say for sure what it might look like, but I do have some preliminary thoughts. I like to write about real people doing real things, with all the difficulties and humor that entails. I also want to learn more about creative organizations and how they are effectively using their internationalists in the world. If yours is such a company, please tell me about it. Thank you—and I look forward to hearing from you.

Catherine Scherer
The Internationalists, LLC
P. O. Box 446
Freeland, WA 98249
E-mail: cwsch@whidbey.com

Notes

Chapter 1

1. Chow Chee Yan, conversation, Kuala Lumpur, Malaysia, October 1997.
2. Stephen K. Rhinesmith, *A Manager's Guide to Globalization,* 2nd edn. (ASTD/Irwin, 1996), p. 24.
3. Danah Zohar, *Rewiring the Corporate Brain* (Berrett-Koehler, 1997).
4. Zohar, *Rewiring the Corporate Brain,* pp. 100–117.
5. Glenn Haldeman, conversation, Denver, Colorado, June 1997.
6. Eduardo Caride, conversation, Buenos Aires, May 1997.
7. Address to Western International Personnel Association, January 1999.

Chapter 2

1. Harvard Business School and AMROP International, *The New International Executive* (1997), p. 22.
2. Susan Vonsild, conversation, Kuala Lumpur, Malaysia, October 1997. Vonsild is managing director of Interlink of Støvring, Denmark.
3. Harvard Business School and AMROP International, *The New International Executive,* p. 18.
4. Tom Fahey, conversation, October 1997. Fahey was formerly vice president of international business, Gates Rubber Company, and vice president, international sales and marketing, General Tire International Company.
5. "America's Best Graduate Schools," *US News and World Report,* March 2, 1998.
6. Cliff Edwards, "Jobs Bountiful for Class of '98," *Denver Post,* May 8, 1998.
7. Linda Sweeney, conversation, New York, September 1997.
8. Chris Murray, conversation, New York, August 1997.

9. Doug Williams, conversation, New York, August 1997.
10. Harvard Business School and AMROP International, *The New International Executive*, p. 14.
11. Selection Research International and National Foreign Trade Council, *International Sourcing and Selection Practices, 1995 Survey Report* (Sept. 1995), p.5.
12. Windham International and National Foreign Trade Council, *Global Relocation Trends, 1996 Survey Report* (1997), p. 21.
13. Ruth Bleuzé, conversation, Boulder, Colorado, May 1998. Dr. Bleuzé is director of assessment and research for Prudential Intercultural Services.
14. Ibid.
15. Harvard Business School and AMROP International, *The New International Executive*, p. 12.
16. Selection Research International and National Foreign Trade Council, *International Sourcing and Selection Practices, 1995 Survey Report* (Sept. 1995), p. 3.
17. Ibid.
18. Harvard Business School and AMROP International, *The New International Executive*, p. 12.
19. Craig Sorti, *The Art of Coming Home* (Intercultural Press, 1997), pp. 1–80.
20. Kevin Taylor, conversation, St. Joseph, Missouri, May 1997.

Chapter 3

1. Geert Hofstede, *Cultures and Organizations: Software of the Mind* (McGraw-Hill, 1997), preface to revised edition.
2. Fons Trompenaars, *Riding the Waves of Culture* (Irwin, 1994), p. 3.
3. Hofstede, *Cultures and Organizations*, pp. 109–138.
4. Trompenaars, *Riding the Waves of Culture*, pp. 33–50.
5. "Bye-bye to Bribes," *US News and World Report*, Dec. 22, 1997, pp. 39–44.
6. Edward T. Hall, *The Dance of Life: The Other Dimension of Time* (Anchor/Doubleday, 1983), pp. 41–53.

7.   Titan Wang, conversation, Taipei, October 1997.

8.   Zohar, *Rewiring the Corporate Brain,* p. 28.

9.   Diane Holt, conversation, Prague, April 1998. Holt is an attorney and consultant, Central European Advisory Group.

10. American Chamber of Commerce in Russia, Membership Survey, September 1988.

11. Transparency International, 1998 Corruption Perception Index.

Chapter 5

1.   Harvard Business School and AMROP International, *The New International Executive,* p. 12.

2.   Jon R. Katzenbach and Douglas K. Smith, "The Discipline of Teams," *Harvard Business Review,* March–April 1993.

3.   Douglas Allen, conversation, Denver, Colorado, September 1997.

4.   Stephen Rhinesmith, *A Manager's Guide to Globalization,* p. 167.

5.   Titan Wang, conversation, Taipei, October 1997.

Bibliography

Books

Althen, Gary. *American Ways: A Guide for Foreigners in the United States*. Intercultural Press, 1988.

Copeland, Lennie, and Lewis Griggs. *Going International: How to Make Friends and Deal Effectively in the Global Marketplace*. Random House, 1995.

Elashmawi, Farid, and Philip R. Harris. *Multi-cultural Management: New Skills for Global Success*. Gulf Publishing, 1993.

Engholm, Christopher. *When Business East Meets Business West: The Guide to Practice and Protocol in the Pacific Rim*. John Wiley & Sons, 1991.

Hall, Edward T. *The Dance of Life: The Other Dimension of Time*. Anchor Press/Doubleday, 1983.

Hall, Edward T. *Beyond Culture*. Anchor Press/Doubleday, 1976.

Hamel, Gary, and C. K. Prahalad. *Competing for the Future*. Harvard Business School Press, 1994.

Hofstede, Geert. *Cultures and Organizations*. McGraw-Hill Book Company Europe, 1991.

Harris, Philip R., and Robert T. Moran. *Managing Cultural Differences*. Gulf Publishing, 1991.

Hoecklin, Lisa. *Managing Cultural Differences: Strategies for Competitive Advantage*. Addison-Wesley, 1995.

Katzenbach, Jon R., and Douglas K. Smith. *The Wisdom of Teams*. Harvard Business School Press, 1993.

Kiersey, David, and Marilyn Bates. *Please Understand Me: Character and Temperament Types*. Promethean Books, 1978.

Koslow, Lawrence E. *Business Abroad*. Gulf Publishing, 1996.

Lipnack, Jessica, and Jeffrey Stamps. *The Age of the Network*. John Wiley & Sons, 1994.

Meyers, Isabelle Briggs. *Gifts Differing: Understanding Personality*. Consulting Psychologists Press, 1980.

Orsburn, Jack D., Linda Moran, Ed Musselwhite, and John H. Zenger. *Self-Directed Work Teams: The New American Challenge*. Irwin Professional Publishing, 1990.

Puchik, Vladimir, Noel M. Tichy, and Carol K. Barnett. *Globalizing Mangement: Creating and Leading a Competitive Organization*. John Wiley & Sons, 1992.

Rhinesmith, Stephen H. *A Manager's Guide to Globalization: Six Keys to Success in a Changing World*. Business ONE Irwin/ASTD, 1993.

Richmond, Yale. *From Da to Yes: Understanding the East Europeans*. Intercultural Press, 1995.

Richmond, Yale. *From Nyet to Da: Understanding the Russians*. Intercultural Press, 1996.

Rosen, Robert. *Leading People, Transforming Business from the Inside Out*. Viking USA. 1996.

Samovan, Larry A., and Richard E. Porter. *Communication Between Cultures*. Wadsworth, 1991.

Scholtes, Peter. *The Team Handbook*. Joiner Associates, 1988.

Seelye, H. Ned, and Alan Seelye-James. *Culture Clash: Managing in a Multicultural World*. NTC BusinessBooks, 1996.

Trompenaars, Fons. *Riding the Waves of Culture: Understanding Diversity in Global Business*. Irwin Professional Publishing, 1994.

Tuller, Lawrence. *Going Global*. Business One Irwin, 1991.

Vaill, Peter B. *Learning as a Way of Being*. Jossey Bass, 1996.

Weeks, William H., Paul B. Pederson, and Richard W. Brislin, eds. *A Manual of Structured Experiences for Cross Cultural Learning*. (SIETAR) Intercultural Press, 1986.

Wellins, Richard S., William C. Byham, and Jeanne M. Wilson. *Empowered Teams*. Jossey-Bass, 1991.

Windham International and National Foreign Trade Council. *Global Relocation Trends 1996 Survey Report*. Windham International, 1997.

Yager, Jan. *Business Protocol: How to Survive and Succeed in Business*. John Wiley & Sons, 1991.

Zohar, Danah. *Rewiring the Corporate Brain*. Berrett-Koehler, 1997.

Articles

Allen, Douglas. "Empowering Expatriates and Organizations to Improve Repatriation Effectiveness." Unpublished manuscript, 1997.

American Chamber of Commerce in Russia. Membership Survey, Sept. 1988 (Internet resource).

"America's Best Graduate Schools." *US News and World Report,* Mar. 2, 1998.

Bartlett, Christopher and Sumantra Gosha. "Managing across Borders." Harvard Business School Press, 1989.

Bennis, Warren. "Leadership in the 21st Century." Training, May 1990.

Bonvillian, Gary, and William A. Nowlin. "Cultural Awareness an Essential Element of Doing Business Abroad." *Business Horizons;* Nov.–Dec. 1994.

Crabb, Steve, and Lynne Brennan. "Worldwide Vision in the Workplace." *People Management,* May 18, 1995.

Edwards, Cliff. "Jobs Bountiful for Class of '98." Associated Press, in *Denver Post,* May 8, 1998.

Gross, Turner and Cedarholm. "Building Teams and Global Operations." *Management Review,* June 1987.

Harvard Business School and Amrop International. "The New International Executive, Business Leadership for the 21st Century." Survey, 1997.

Iles, Paul. "Learning to Work with Difference (Challenging Learning)." *Personnel Review,* Sept. 1995.

International Monetary Fund. Staff Survey. "World Economic Outlook." World Wide Web posting, May 1997.

Joinson, Carla. "Cultural Sensitivity Makes Good Business Sense." *HR Magazine,* Nov. 1995.

Kaipa, Prasad, and Steve Johnson. "Unlearning: Breaking Out of the Box." In their *Igniting Your Natural Genius.* (Internet Resource; The Mithya Institute.)

Katz, Jan Hack. "Cultural Issues in International Business." In *Handbook of International Business,* edited by Ingo Walter and Tracy Murray. John Wiley & Sons, 1988.

Katzenbach, Jon R., and Douglas K. Smith. "The Discipline of Teams." *Harvard Business Review,* March–April 1993.

Laabs, Jennifer J. "HR Pioneers Explore the Road Less Traveled." Workforce Online (Internet Resource).

McCain, Barbara. "Multicultural Team Learning: An Approach towards Communication Competency." *Management Decision,* Nov. 1994.

McKenna, Stephen. "The Business Impact of Management Attitudes towards Dealing with Conflict: A Cross-Cultural Assessment." *Journal of Managerial Psychology*, July 1995.

Moyes, Jeremy. Review of Nicola Phillips, *Managing International Teams. Academy of Management Executives*, August 1994.

Omestad, Thomas. "Bye-bye to Bribes." *US News and World Report,* December 1997.

Pearson, Andrall E. "Corporate Redemption and the Seven Deadly Sins." *Harvard Business Review,* May–June 1992.

Perlmutter, Howard V., and David A. Herman. "Cooperate to Compete Globally." Harvard Business Review; March–April 1986.

Solomon, Charlene Marmer. "Repatriation: Up, Down or Out?" Workforce Online (Internet resource).

Solomon, Charlene Marmer. "Navigating Your Search for Global Talent." Workforce Online (Internet resource).

Watson, W. E., K. Kamalesh, and L. K. Michaelsen. "Cultural Diversity's Impact on Group Process and Performance: Comparing Culturally Homogeneous and Culturally Diverse Task Groups." Working paper, 1996.

White, Cheryl. "Models for Quality System Implementation in Change Resistant Organizations." Abstract prepared for the Rocky Mountain Quality Conference, 1997.

White, Cheryl. "Measuring Change Resistance in Change Resistant Organizations." Unpublished paper, May, 1996.

World Trade Organization. "International Trade Trends and Statistics." Prepared by the Economic Research and Analysis Division and the Statistics and Information Systems Division (Internet resource), 1995.

INDEX

A

adaptability, 14, 63-65
affiliative cultures, 67-72
Alaska Seafood Marketing Institute, 176
AMROP International, see Harvard-AMROP study
Armstrong, Bob, 104-108
Argentina, 64, 109-112
Asia, cultural differences, 6, 9-10, 66-67; see also specific countries
assessment and evaluation, 35
    instruments and tests, 39-41
assignment, 42-45
    rotational, 42-43
authority, attitudes toward, 65-67, 159
autonomy, 14-15

B

Becton-Dickinson and Co., 96-99
Bleuzé, Ruth, 35-36
boards, corporate, 25
body language, 81-82
Brazil, 67, 74, 77, 80, 100-108
bribery and corruption, 75-76, 91-92

C

career development and planning, 28-29
Caride, Eduardo, 15, 109-112
cells of excellence model, 105
Central Europe, 87
change, attitudes toward, 63
children, 41-42
China, 66, 71, 72, 85, 124-128
Citibank of Argentina, 109
Citizens Democracy Corps (CDC), 142
coaching, see mentors

D

H

I

island models, 61-62
Italy, 113-116

J

Japan, 66, 70, 71, 72

K

Kabelkom, 117
Katzenbach, Jon, 150
Kawahara, Doug, 96-99
Korea, 82

L

language, see also communication
    element of culture, 78
    English as common, 178
    training, 143-146
Latin America, 70, 71, 74, 77
laws, attitudes toward, 73-74
leadership, 153-155
    creative, 13, 49-50
    project, 3-4, 5-6, 13
Leaf North America (Hershey), 124-128
logistics, 15

M

Malaysia, 66, 69, 70, 77-78, 83
management
    styles, 63, 65, 67, 68
    training, 140-141
market economy, 133
market research, 15-16, 124-128
maxims, 183
mentors and coaches, 44, 148-150, 177
    home-based, 45-46, 48
    returned internationalists, 44

Mexico, 64
Meyers Briggs Type Indicator (MBTI), 39-40
mobility, 63
Murray, Chris, 33

N

National Foreign Trade Council (NFTC), 35, 37
negotiating style, 80; see also communication
Netherlands, 96-99
networked cultures, 9
Newtonian cultures, 9

O

Out-and-In process, 47
Overseas Assignment Inventory (OAI), 40

P

P'an, Virginia, 124-128
partners, local, 12, 91, 130, 148-150, 172
pause, conversational, 79
Pavlenko, Victor, 129-136
Peace Corps, 40
peer exchanges, 143
personal relationships, see affiliation; socializing
Peters, Jim, 113-116
politeness, 78-84; see also deference
Prudential Intercultural Services, 35

R

Racimec, 100-103
recruitment, 30-42
    entry-level, 11, 31
    foreign, 33-34
    internal, 11, 25-26, 35-38
relocation assistance, 44
    costs, 148

repatriation , 46-52
rewiring the brain, 86
Rhinesmith, Stephen K., 6
risk-taking, 63
Rocha, Antonio-Carlos, 100-103
Rotary International, Group Study Exchange, 141
rotational assignments, 146-147
rules, attitudes toward, 63-65, 73-74
Russia, 129-136; see also Soviet Union
Russia Telecommunication Development Corp., 129-136

S

Samsonite, 113-116
Santa Elina Mines, 104-108
selection, see assessment; partners; recruitment
Selection Research International (SRI), 35
silence, 80
Smith, Douglas, 150
socializing, 69, 114, 121
Soviet Union and satellites, former, 86-93, 118-123
    ethnic conflicts, 89
spouses, 41-42
Star Team process, 152
stereotypes, 57-58
strategies, 10-18
Sweeney, Linda, 51, 117-123

T

Taiwan, 69, 72, 85, 156
Taylor, Kevin, 48
TCI Cable, 117
teams, international, 150-163
    behavior, 80
    case studies, 99-127
    protocols, 162
Telefónica de Argentina, 109-112
Telefónica de España, 109-112

W

Wang, Titan, 85, 157
Western cultures, characteristics of, 9-10
Williams, Doug, 33
Windham International, 35
women, see gender
World Trade Center, 142
Worldwide Partners, 167-179

Y

Yan, Chow Chee, 5, 158
YTONG, 175

Z

Zohar, Danah, 6, 9, 86

About the author

Catherine Scherer has combined expertise in international management consulting, corporate restructuring, marketing, and business development over a thirty-year career. She has served as vice president and as director of professional services for an international career development firm, working closely with industries including telecommunications, petroleum, mining, aerospace, utilities, manufacturing, health care, consumer products, and high-tech. She has managed complex restructuring projects providing direction, coordination, program design, and delivery for both Fortune 500 companies and smaller organizations.

Ms. Scherer has consulted with executives, managers, and professionals on career issues and has presented and facilitated cross-cultural training programs for expatriate executives and their families. She has designed a specialized career management program for returning expatriates, addressing dual-career issues. She has authored training program guides, articles, and manuals. As a keynote speaker and trainer, she has addressed business audiences in several countries.

An avid interculturalist, Ms. Scherer lived for ten years in Europe, where she coordinated and marketed multiple-site educational programs for an American college doing business with the U.S. military. She was responsible for recruiting and staffing at fifteen geographically separated sites, providing counseling and training for staff and students.

Ms. Scherer holds a degree in education and social sciences, with additional studies in business and economics. She has completed graduate studies in psychology and enjoys pursuing continuing education.

She is an active member of Rotary International, the International Institute of Human Resources, Society for Human Resources Management, and Western International Personnel Association. She has served on the boards of several professional and service organizations.

To order additional copies of

The Internationalists

Book: $24.95   Shipping/Handling: $3.50

Contact: ***BookPartners, Inc.***
P.O. Box 922
Wilsonville, OR 97070

E-mail: bpbooks@teleport.com
Fax: 503-682-8684
Phone: 503-682-9821
Order: 1-800-895-7323

Visit our web site:
www.bookpartners.com